**LEARNING FROM
CYBER-SAVVY STUDENTS**

LEARNING FROM CYBER-SAVVY STUDENTS

How Internet-Age Kids
Impact Classroom Teaching

Anne Hird

STERLING, VIRGINIA

Published in 2000 by

Stylus Publishing, LLC
22883 Quicksilver Drive
Sterling, Virginia 20166

Library of Congress Cataloging-in-Publication Data
Hird, Anne, 1959–
    Learning from cyber-savvy students : how Internet-age kids impact
classroom teaching / Anne Hird.
        p. cm.
    Includes bibliographical references and index.
    ISBN 1-57922-030-4 (alk. paper)—ISBN 1-57922-031-2
(paper : alk. paper)
        1. Internet in education—Case studies. 2. Teacher-student
relationships—Case studies. I. Title.

LB1028.43 .H57 2000
373.133'44678—dc21
                                                                00-057375

First edition, 2000
Hard cover ISBN: 1-57922-030-4
Paperback ISBN: 1-57922-031-2

Printed in the United States of America

Printed on acid free paper

For Internet-Age Kids

CONTENTS

ACKNOWLEDGMENTS

This study was possible only through the cooperation of students and teachers at Cityview School. When I first introduced myself to the students, one girl looked at me quizzically and wanted to know why I would bother doing this research. My purpose for the study at the same time was to inform classroom teaching as the world becomes, in the words of another student, "more Internet-oriented." I am grateful to the students who have helped to provide a glimpse of what their online world looks like to them.

My heartfelt appreciation goes out to Rhode Island College and University of Rhode Island faculty, especially my advisor, John J. Gleason, and dissertation committee members, Bill Holland, Cheryl McCarthy, and Betty Young. I am greatly indebted to Rhode Island College and the Beneficent Congregational Society's Lucinda Maxfield Fund for the financial support that enabled me to devote the time necessary for this ethnographic study.

Most of all, I appreciate the unwavering support my family has given me. My husband, Jonathan, has provided steady encouragement, always comparing my progress to the mile marks in a marathon. Erica and Alison have helped me to keep my sense of humor and have been a constant reminder of the need to listen to student voices.

Pseudonyms are used for both the school and participants throughout this text. No attempt was made to match pseudonym with the ethnicity of the individual student, in part to protect the anonymity of participants and in part because this book does not explore ethnic differences in Internet use. Staff members are not distinguished by role, nor do personal pronouns used in the text necessarily correspond with the sex of the staff member. Again, this is to protect participants' anonymity.

Students' comments have been edited only for purposes of clarity. Messages posted by students on the Web-based bulletin board established for this study appear here as they appeared on the computer screen. Students' screen names have been replaced with pseudonyms, again to protect anonymity.

Students frequently used commercial names for Internet-related products and services. These names have been replaced with the corresponding generic term wherever it was possible to do so without changing the meaning of the speaker's comment.

Anne Hird

I

INTRODUCTION

Children, Adults, and the Thinking Machine

It's not new to us, but when, when they [adults] were growing up, computers were like, like large rooms that could calculate one plus one in like a couple of hours, and you know . . . they never get to see these things. . . . They hear about this thing that isn't a human but it can think and it's like a new concept. . . .
—Student

In an era in which children can traverse the globe on the Internet before they are allowed to leave the backyard on a bicycle, it is difficult to remember back less than a decade to a time when the Internet was a little-known domain of computer scientists and researchers. In 1993, I registered for my first email account and proceeded to learn how to use what was then an unattractive, cumbersome text-based medium. At that time, I understood the Internet primarily as a faster, more convenient substitute for telephone communication and fax or postal transfer of documents. Colleagues and friends speculated that this latest innovation might soon take its place alongside the Beta videocassette player as a short-lived, trendy technology. It was not until almost a year later that I first sensed that the Internet might have a far greater impact than this on our daily lives.

Early in 1994, I was organizing a professional development program for school librarians and teachers. The plan was to provide hands-on instruction to familiarize educators with text-based, command-driven Internet functions. After a meeting at the nearby university computing lab, in which the workshop would take place, a computer center staff member invited the workshop speakers and me up to her office. She was excited about a new Internet-based program and wanted to show it to us. As she clicked on her computer mouse, the screen was transformed from a string of gray text to a full-color graphic interface. Displayed on the monitor was the score of a championship soccer game being played at that very moment on another continent. Flags of all the nations competing in the championship formed a colorful border around the screen. By simply pointing and clicking with the mouse, the user could move on to other screens to view more pictures and detailed information about the soccer championship.

What we were looking at was Mosaic, the first "point and click" Internet browsing software. Soon, Internet users would no longer need to know any special command language. After a momentary silence, my astonished colleagues proceeded to ask a variety of technical questions about this new development. In those few seconds of silence, I realized I was witnessing a significant development. There was no sound, video, or animation yet, but still this precursor to Netscape provided easy access to highly attractive, up-to-the-minute information on an event taking place hundreds of miles away. At the time, I had no idea what the possible implications of this technology were, but I suddenly had the sense that the Internet was going to have far-reaching impact. Before long, schools, businesses, and homes were connecting to the Information Superhighway. Within five years after the United States National Science Foundation lifted restrictions prohibiting commercial use of the Internet, this technology has allowed for dramatic changes in the way we work and play.

The World Wide Web has become a global marketplace, where companies large and small entice consumers to purchase everything from pharmaceuticals to automobiles. Almost every television commercial now carries a Web address where consumers can get more information about or purchase the product. Web-based auctions, which enable Internet users to buy or sell items ranging from sports memorabilia to computer hardware, serve as an electronic counterpart to the open-air street market. Although most small corner markets were displaced long ago by enormous discount supermarkets, the delivery service once provided by young boys on bicycles has recently reappeared. Internet users can now browse through the "aisles" of an online grocery store, place an order, and have it delivered to the door at a specified time. Consumer purchasing power increases as comparison shopping requires only a few quick clicks of the mouse, rather than hours of phoning or driving around town for the best prices. In just a few short years, e-commerce has become a critical factor in the overall state of international economic stability.

The workplace is rapidly changing, as more and more information is moved around in electronic formats. Online job listings enable employers to reach a far wider audience than the newspaper classified advertisements did. Prospective employees, in turn, use powerful online searching tools to locate quickly and efficiently available positions that match their skills, desired geographical location, and salary range. Roles are changing as the combined use of email and voice mail at the managerial and executive levels free up office receptionists to assume new responsibilities. Similarly, banking institutions are hiring more computer operators and fewer traditional tellers to keep pace with a shift toward online banking. Nurses are now being trained to supplement home visits by monitoring housebound patients' conditions via telecommunications. Home office furniture sales have soared as employees in a range of occupations take advantage of telecommunications to work at home.

The entertainment industry is undergoing dramatic change, with teens leading the way. The recent release of MP3 and "writable" compact disc technology allows a music fan to download popular music files and create customized compact discs. The choice of songs to include on a single disc has shifted from music producer to consumer. Games ranging from classic board games to casino gambling are now available online, eliminating the need for players to organize face-to-face meetings with competitors. Moviegoers no longer need to visit a cinema to see previews of an upcoming Hollywood release; Web sites now provide advance publicity for major Hollywood releases. Television networks have formed partnerships with Internet-related industries to maintain high-powered Web-interactive Web sites. If a television viewer misses the evening news, the person can always check up on the day's events on the network's Web site. The added advantage online is that the selection of news reports and the depth of detail on any event become the Internet user's choice. Online, there is no need to listen through the local news and weather in order to get to the sports report; instead, the news "viewer" can click directly on the sports report.

Amid all this change, many educators were not immediately convinced that the Internet would have any more impact on classroom teaching and learning than did the old filmstrip projectors and record players, which already cluttered school storerooms. After more than a decade, the microcomputer itself had had little effect on classroom learning; why would adding modems to the computers make a difference? One of the distinctions is the degree to which this innovation has permeated children's lives outside school. Out-of-school Internet access is not limited to teens with home computers. Public libraries, community centers, friends' homes, and parents' workplaces are among the many other locations where students can get online. Whereas the computer once held special status as an expensive technical innovation for prior generations, it is merely another household appliance for today's teens. For youth growing up in the Internet Age, this latest innovation, which combines computers and telecommunications, carries no more mystique than the telephone or refrigerator.

Outside school, students are using the Internet for almost every activity imaginable. Whereas their parents were advised as children not to cross busy main streets, today's youth are using telecommunications to cross continents and oceans. On the Internet, they can work and play with peers physically located anywhere in the world. They know their online friends by email address, not by face. Their teachers and parents believe that email has replaced the telephone as one of the major distractions from homework. Today's teens are just as likely to hang out in online chat rooms as they are to cruise indoor shopping malls in search of social activity. In the same way that their parents once swapped baseball cards, these youngsters trade computer game files online. Whereas their parents built lofty towers and bridges out of wooden blocks, Internet-Age children construct Web sites out of bits of digitized information. The dress-up games played by prior generations take on a whole new meaning as young adolescents use screen names online to test out or try on different aspects of their personalities.

As banks, medical centers, government agencies, libraries, retail vendors, and other major institutions are rapidly changing how they do business to keep pace with the surge in Internet use, schools continue to lag far behind. Outside school, children and teens are constantly discovering new ways to use the Internet that may not necessarily fit with their classroom learning. In school, both the range and sequence of topics to be studied are usually predetermined by the curriculum or textbook. On the Internet, children's learning is driven by their curiosity as they pursue links from one Web site to another. In the classroom, the teacher is in charge, particularly when it comes to classroom communication. The teacher determines when, to whom, and about what students may speak. On the Internet, children and teens negotiate among themselves and self-enforce the rules for participation in any given Web site. School learning is an orderly affair, organized so that discrete learning activities fit into each class period and the whole class moves together through the curriculum at relatively the same pace. On the Internet, students find learning to be a messy process as their pursuit of any given topic takes unanticipated twists and turns.

What happens when cyber-savvy students enter the classroom? How does classroom use of this innovation fit with students' out-of-school Internet use? Will students coming into school with a full range of Internet experience influence how computer technology is used in the classroom? Given that children growing up with this technology may approach it differently from the adults around them (Turkle, 1995, p. 78), the students' own perspectives are critical to understanding how students use the Internet in their school learning. With hopes of gaining a better understanding of how youth are learning in this new online world, I spent six months observing and interviewing eighth-grade students at Cityview School. What interested me most was how these students fit their experience on the Internet with their classroom learning, given that school as an institution long predates this technological innovation. My assumption was always that these teens may be our single best untapped resource for understanding better how they might use this technology in school.

In order to understand how students use the Internet in the class-room, I needed to locate a school that had moved past the widely known logistical obstacles to educational computer use. My purpose was to explore how students use the Internet in a classroom with adequate support for computer technology use. I had three criteria for identifying a setting:

1. The school had to have adequate hardware, software, technical support, and professional development to minimize the lack of any of these as interfering variables.

2. Internet use had to be required for all students to complete their courses successfully.

3. Internet use had to occur naturally, in contrast to situations in which university or other external research projects drove school technology use.

In the year that I spent searching for a site, I learned that few schools met these criteria. I discovered two predominant patterns of student computer use in schools. Many schools require all students to take a basic computer course, but students have little access to school computers outside this class. In other schools, a few exemplary teachers provide their students with extensive access to computers. In other words, either all the students have a little access or a few students have extensive access. Very few schools have the hardware, software, technical support, professional development, and administrative leadership needed to support extensive computer use by all students. Cityview School stands out as an exception, having moved past many of the widely recognized logistical obstacles to classroom computer use.

Cityview School is a small, private independent school that serves 130 students in grades four through eight.[1] Its mission is "to challenge minority and low-income children to succeed in college preparatory high school programs and to become community leaders." Cityview's Internet use is not typical of the schools that I contacted or visited. Teachers and students at Cityview have access to more technological resources than currently found in many American schools. Cityview School has had computers in its classrooms since 1992. Early computer use consisted almost entirely of word processing for student writing assignments. In 1994, the school developed a long-term technology plan extending into the year 2005 and then began fund-raising for implementation. By 1996, Cityview had secured grants and private donations totaling $50,000 to install a buildingwide network and three state-of-the-art computers in every classroom, allowing for a one to six ratio of computers to students. Peripheral equipment—including printers, a scanner, and a digital camera, along with utility (e.g., word-processing) and educational software—were purchased. The school subscribed to an educational Internet service provider. Students can now access the Internet from any computer in the building.

Absent at Cityview are the barriers most frequently cited as impediments to school technology use. The school's administration has adopted technology as a high priority and follows through with the support teachers need to use computers in the classroom. The leadership's commitment extends well beyond rhetoric and token efforts to satisfy public pressure for students to use computers. Administrators aggressively pursue grants, solicit private donations of cash and equipment, and include technology expenses in the school's operating budget.

Cityview has always had some form of technical support. The school now funds a half-time staff position for computer maintenance and instruction, which is, in one teacher's words, ". . . a fairly significant commitment for a school of 135 kids." The Cityview administration recognizes that professional development related to classroom technology use usually falls far short of the need and is seeking out continued opportunities for faculty to learn how to use computers in the classroom. Teachers have attended workshops and received on-site assistance through a partnership with a local university. Cityview's future plans include supporting a staff member to pursue a master's degree in educational technology, so that the school has a technology curriculum specialist on staff.

The flexible approach to time and space use that Cityview adopted long ago to accommodate its project-based curriculum is conducive to student technology use. Teachers at Cityview meet regularly to plan student research projects. As part of the planning process, teachers evaluate past Internet use and discuss new strategies to integrate the technology into future projects. The school's flexible daily schedule allows students to see simple Internet tasks through to completion and to take on larger projects that would not fit into customary 50-minute class periods. Students are trusted and encouraged to move freely about the building to use any available space to work on their projects. The same strategy for providing students with adequate space to practice speeches, design posters, and rehearse plays is applied to computer use. If all computers in one classroom are in use, students use idle computers in other classrooms and administrative offices. On one occasion, I went looking for the assistant principal, only to discover that he had turned over his desk and computer to a student for the class period. Even though each classroom has only three computers, as many as 10 to 12 students per class can use the Internet simultaneously.

Cityview's curriculum emphasizes interdisciplinary thematic units designed to "promote coherent and compelling learning." The interdisciplinary projects on topics students themselves identify are an ideal match for the constructivist learning afforded by computer technology (Means & Olson, 1995, p. 160). One Cityview faculty member explained that, on each project, teachers require students to

> . . . [identify] in their research paper a Web site that they really used as a resource just as much as any article or any book and that was one that they really went into in depth and tried to pull out whatever information they could get from that one . . . Web site.

Student Internet use extends across classes, ranging from social studies to drama and art. No one teacher is left sacrificing instruction in a single content area to provide all the "technical overhead"—that is, the technical skills students need to use the computer as a learning tool (Means & Olson, 1995, p. 168).

The school's status as a relatively new independent school is conducive to change. One faculty member compared the school as an organization to a developing teenager:

> . . . When you're 13, you're in your adolescence. . . . Your identity is really beginning to emerge. You're stabilizing a bit. The acne is clearing up, hopefully at some point soon, and you kind of get through, and that's where I think Cityview is at. I think

we're kind of struggling with, "Who are we? What's our curriculum look like? What's our staffing and how do we deal with this? How do we deal with that?"

Neither the school as an institution nor the relatively young faculty has decades-old routines into which the technology use must fit (Kerr, 1991, p. 120; Olson, 1988). As an independent school, the site is not bound by the layers of bureaucratic constraints faced by many public schools, so it has the ability to act quickly on desired curriculum changes. According to the same teacher, these factors combined to form an ideal climate for the introduction of the Internet and related computer technology:

> We pulled the staff together to share vision. We had leadership that was in place and ready to go and I think that was the key. And then we were able to deliver a product that was solid and that enabled us to attract the funds, and that enabled us to keep pushing to bring it faster. . . .

Teachers and students alike recognize the school as being ahead of others in its computer technology use. A faculty member who had apologized for what he perceived as underutilization of technology later returned from a statewide teachers' meeting feeling differently. Other teachers statewide, the Cityview teacher said, ". . . weren't doing *anything.*" Students, too, have noted the emphasis their school places on technology and have predicted that their school computer use would decline when they move on to area high schools.

Participants in this study are 34 eighth-grade students in two interdisciplinary social studies classes that emphasize the research skills students need to succeed in college preparatory high schools. All students are required by teachers to use the Internet for their research projects. Students have daily access to the Internet via school computers during classes and recess, as well as before and after school. Cityview's acceptable Internet use policy states that, "Students use the network to conduct research and communicate with others" for educational purposes. Students are held responsible for complying with "[g]eneral school rules for behavior" and are expected to ". . . act in a considerate and responsible manner" while using computers. The policy does not prohibit the use of any particular technical function of the Internet (e.g., chat rooms), and it includes provisions for students to use email. (See Appendix A, "Cityview School Acceptable Internet Use Policy.")

The students' Internet experience as observed and self-reported ranges from beginner to one expert user, who provides technical assistance to online friends. Interviews revealed that students learn Internet-related technical skills in a variety of ways. Students' strategies for learning how to use this technology include trial and error, collaboration with friends both online and offline,[2] online help screens, print computer manuals, and occasional questions asked of a teacher. Although only 11 of the 34 students have home Internet access, 25 report using the Internet from a variety of locations outside school. For students whose families subscribe to an Internet service provider, access is not always consistent. Obstacles to home use cited by these students include parental restrictions, competition with other family members for online time, and unresolved technical problems.

None of the Cityview students spends excessive amounts of time online. The majority of students (24 of the 34) estimate that they use the Internet one to three times per week. Only two students say that they use the Internet more than eight times weekly. The most fluent users indicated in interviews that their heaviest use is on weekends, when they typically spend two to three hours a day online. Cityview students' online activities and relationships constitute only one aspect of their busy lives; other demands, including school, homework, and extracurricular activities, limit the time they spend on the Internet.

Over a six-month period, I observed these students working both online and away from computers on classroom projects for which Internet use was required. I interviewed students individually and in small groups. Although my goal was to learn directly from the students themselves how they use the Internet in school, I interviewed Cityview staff to learn what their expectations were for classroom Internet use. In order to gain a vantage point from which to observe students online, I set up a Web-based discussion forum for students to reflect on how they use the Internet. Additional data sources included students' completed research papers and Web sites.

My initial approach was to collect the words and phrases children use to describe their Internet use and to analyze this data for indications of constructivist learning.³ The language used to describe a technology indicates the degree to which a particular society embraces the innovation. Initially, adults often reinforce existing institutional practices by applying the new technology to past practices. They do not attempt new tasks made possible by the innovation (Bailey, 1996; Duffy & Cunningham, 1996; Papert, 1993). Phrases such as "information superhighway" and "home page" reflect a tendency to describe an innovation in terms of familiar concepts, even though these terms fall short of accurately and completely representing the innovation (Bailey, 1996). Children may not follow this pattern, because they do not have a firmly established set of "old ideas" onto which to graft the new technology.

I quickly learned that Cityview students have no special lexicon to describe their Internet use. When students describe their online activities and relationships, they use no special language to distinguish between their technology-mediated experiences on the Internet and activities and conversations that occur offline in places such as their school and homes. Outside of school, students move very fluidly between their online and offline lives, using the Internet for everything from swapping computer game files to designing collaborative Web sites across hundreds of miles. For students, the value of the Internet as a learning tool lies in online communication around shared information. If used as these students understand it, the Internet does not fit *into* the classroom; rather, there is a need to build bridges between the classroom and dynamic new online learning environments.

In comparing what the students know they can do with the Internet with how they use it in school, I discovered that Cityview students' knowledge of the Internet extends far beyond their classroom use of this new technology. With the exception of six boys who designed their own Web sites, the students' classroom Internet use is limited to searching the Web for information related to school projects and assignments. In school, these teens do not question either implicit or explicit limits on their classroom Internet use, even though they believe that they understand the Internet better than their teachers do. When students come into the classroom, they set aside their out-of-school Internet experience and honor their teachers' understanding of the innovation. Even in a school that is considered to be highly progressive and student-centered, the students do not see it as their place to lead their teachers into the 21ˢᵗ century. What is needed is a new approach to professional development that accounts for a paradox that these students recognize: teachers are being asked to teach with a cognitive tool with which they have had little or no prior experience as learners. Until teachers become fluent online learners alongside their students, schools run the risk of becoming increasingly irrelevant to students growing up in the Internet Age.

Notes

1. The student population is 42% African American, 27% Caucasian, 11% biracial, 10% Latino, and 10% Asian American. Ninety percent of the students receive half to full scholarships (as reported by the school in November 1997).

2. *Online* is used to describe activities and relationships which are mediated by the combination of microcomputer and telecommunications technology that constitutes the Internet as a technical entity. *Offline* refers to direct experience not mediated by Internet technology.

3. Constructivist pedagogy rests on the assumption that, outside the individual learner's mind, there does not exist a set body of knowledge to be acquired; rather, knowledge is constructed through the learner's struggle to solve complex problems and is tested for compatibility with the understandings of others (Perkins, 1992; von Glaserfeld, 1996).

2

NEW POSSIBILITIES FOR
LEARNING

THE PROMISE OF THE INTERNET

. . . I mean there is something very attractive about using it . . .
you can kind of sense it.
                          —A teacher on students using the Internet

Since the early 1980s, computer technology has fueled the imagination of educators. With little more than a vague sense that computers would be necessary to prepare students for the 21st century, school
districts allocated millions of dollars toward computer purchases.
Microcomputers were introduced into classrooms with the promise of
revolutionizing education; instead, they became closely aligned with
one of the underlying purposes of school: to move students through a
predetermined curriculum with the greatest efficiency possible. As the
decade of the microcomputer drew to a close, there was little perceptible change in student learning, and the initial enthusiasm surrounding
school use of computers waned. Computer labs were not maintained or
upgraded and, in many schools, fell into disuse. The computer may
have allowed for increased volume and speed in school learning, but it
fell far short of the promise of bringing about fundamental changes in
classroom teaching and learning.

Outside schools, however, computer technology continued to develop and proliferate at a rate that seemed difficult to keep pace with. Each successive computer model was more powerful than the last, as the technology was refined to allow more information to be processed at ever-faster rates of speed. In 1993, public access to the Internet, which wedded the information functions of the microcomputer with telecommunications technology, created a whole new set of possibilities. By 1997, the Internet had gained enough economic and political momentum to prompt United States President Bill Clinton to declare that every school in America should be wired for Internet use by the year 2000. A year later, Great Britain's Prime Minister Tony Blair established 2002 as the goal for connecting all schools to its National Grid for Learning, a government-sponsored clearinghouse for Internet-based learning resources. Teachers might well question the reinvestment of millions of precious education dollars in a technology that had already failed once to have significant impact on classroom learning.

This second wave of school computer use gets its momentum from the promise that the Internet will extend learning far beyond the traditional time and place boundaries of the classroom. In the early 1990s, the convergence of several technological developments resulted in the widespread availability of the Internet as a complex system of computers and telecommunications that connects computer networks worldwide. The Internet had been in use and under continual development by a small group of American research institutions and government agencies for almost three decades. The 1990 release of the World Wide Web by Switzerland's CERN physics laboratory provided the technical capacity for the highly appealing multimedia functions now associated with the Internet. In 1993, Mosaic became the first point and click Internet browsing software, eliminating the need for Internet users to know any special computer command language. At the same time that these technical advances simplified Internet use, the National Science Foundation in the United States lifted sanctions prohibiting Internet use for commercial purposes. Internet use spread from research institutions to businesses, private households, libraries, and schools.

Prior to the introduction of the Internet, school computer use was contained within the classroom or computer lab and did little to alleviate the isolation that characterizes classrooms. Ironically, it became common to find a $2,000 computer installed in a classroom that still lacked a $25 telephone. When school was in session, students and teachers continued to have little, if any, connection with the world outside the classroom. In most schools, computers enhanced but did not substantially change classroom teaching and learning. Programmed learning, for example, allowed teachers to monitor more closely and precisely students' progress as "skill and drill" exercises shifted from conventional paper workbook to self-correcting computer programs. If computers failed to function, as often happened, students and teachers could and did continue to pursue the same learning goals and objectives without the computer.

The Internet is inherently different from other communications technologies previously used in the classroom. Educational radio and television, which fell into disuse soon after the initial novelty wore off, were both one-directional broadcast media, with the capacity for the dissemination of information only. These technologies allowed the teacher to bring information from remote sources into the classroom, but they did not alter either the teacher's responsibility for delivering information to students or the students' role as passive recipients of that information. In fact, educational television was so closely aligned with the teacher's role as conveyor of information that some teachers feared losing their jobs. If televised instruction to large numbers of students proved to be effective, it could replace the more personalized but far less cost-efficient instruction they provided (Cuban, 1986).

In contrast, the Internet was designed specifically to encourage collaboration among scientists and engineers at major American research institutions. One of the primary features of the Internet is the capacity for multidirectional communication and transfer of information. For almost three decades, this system of interconnected computer networks has provided a means for researchers at select institutions to exchange their findings and simultaneously discuss the shared data. Once the Internet was made available to anyone with a computer and telephone line, it grew rapidly to include 148 million users worldwide by the end of 1998 (Big Picture Geographics, 1999). The Internet took on the allure of a virtual theme park, as new technical developments enabled users to send, receive, and manipulate for their own purposes audio and video files, as well as text and still graphic documents. The endless possibilities seemed too good to be true. An Internet user could get weather forecasts for any region of the world, listen to popular music, catch up on television or radio news, create and send animated email greeting cards, order prescription medicine, and sell a used automobile, all from a single computer. Before long, schools were faced with the question of how to keep pace with a new generation of students, who knew their favorite Web addresses as well as they knew the alphabet.

Although we are still in the early stages of discovering uses for Internet technology, new possibilities for learning online abound. At one level, the Internet serves as a vast electronic library. Using the World Wide Web, teachers and students can get information on any topic imaginable in just seconds. The volume and diversity of readily accessible online information far exceed that of the information previously available in the books, periodicals, CD-ROMs and other resources physically contained within any one school. This access to and manageability of information permit learners to pursue a broad spectrum of open-ended projects (Papert, 1996, p. 113). Learning is no longer restricted by the information resources available in the classroom or school library; instead, the student's imagination is the only limiting factor for the range of topics explored.

Textbooks become obsolete as computer software brings to life concepts that are not easily learned from conventional text descriptions. Using e-toys soon to be available on a Disney Web site, for example, a child can design a car and a steering wheel to control the car's movement across a computer screen. The child quickly discovers the need to alter the gear ratio between the car and steering wheel to gain optimum control of the vehicle. This use of computer technology provides children with a representation of the concepts related to ratios and fractions that is far more powerful than current textbook discussions (Kay, 1998). Within the next 10 years, the combination of computer and telecommunications technology will enable schools to provide learning experiences in which the student's role shifts from passive observer to lead actor. Instead of reading about glaciers, a student may become immersed in a simulation in which the learner is hovering above a moving glacier in the year 2000 B.C. The student may discover that "glacial speed" is actually much more perceptible than a text description conveys (Tiffin & Rajasingham, 1995, pp. 14–15).

Schools in many cultures are responsible for children's personal growth as well as for their students' reading, writing, and mathematical reasoning skills. The Internet provides low-risk settings for personal development. In online environments such as chat rooms, an Internet user can assume a screen name or pseudonym to experiment with multiple aspects of the individual's personality in nonthreatening ways. The process of learning in a virtual environment might be compared to multitasking in the Windows environment. Online, an individual can maintain a variety of personalities, each of which can be "open" or "closed", under development or on hold, in a way similar to the manipulation of windows on the microcomputer (Turkle, 1995). A student who is usually reserved in classroom discussion, for example, might feel freer to express an opinion online. In other cases, Internet users are able to participate in professional dialogue free of assumptions or prejudices associated with each speaker's gender, race, age, or physical appearance.

The Internet may be used as a safe environment for learning new life skills. One young woman learned to "live" on the Internet as a disabled person for several months before she was physically able to go out into the real world in her new condition as an amputee. As she moved in and out of chat rooms, the woman encountered, in a risk-free setting, virtual versions of the challenges she could expect in real life (Turkle, 1995). In another example, patients scheduled to travel to the Fred Hutchinson Cancer Research Center in Seattle for bone marrow transplants will soon be able to tour the hospital, familiarize themselves with the surrounding neighborhood, attend medical lectures, and meet staff and other transplant patients prior to leaving home. These and other features of an interactive, three-dimensional Web site being developed by Microsoft are designed to alleviate the fears and stresses most frequently experienced by new patients (Stone, 1998).

Some of these applications exist independent of the Internet, but the computer hardware and software needed to take advantage of these new learning tools is far too expensive for most schools. The Internet provides a means for the widespread, affordable distribution of sophisticated computer programs not likely to be found in any single school. Over time, the Internet may be used to make powerful artificial intelligence programs and associated expertise available in the classroom.

Everyday use of artificial intelligence tools, once reserved for the highest-level scientists and engineers, may lead to radical changes in learning, so that human thought comes to focus on patterns. The power and proliferation of computers are such that an enormous amount of data is now available to an individual. The potential exists for computers to identify patterns in the data, through simultaneously occurring calculations. Learning then breaks away from sequential thinking to emphasize the significance of more fluid, simultaneously occurring patterns (Bailey, 1996). In a very early example, Lewis Richardson collected data on armed conflicts ranging in magnitude from individual murders to World Wars I and II, all of which took place between 1820 and 1949. The Scottish physicist/psychologist then performed a series of mathematical computations on this data to project accurately the course the international arms race would take through the 1960s (pp. 101–108).

Online distribution of these new computational tools allows children to use artificial intelligence systems to explore complex problems. In research at the Massachusetts Institute of Technology's Media Lab, children use StarLogo programming language to direct multiple objects on a computer screen to move simultaneously. Children program each object, or "car," to move according to a few simple rules similar to those that govern highway driving, such as direction and speed limit. Children then study the "traffic jam" patterns that emerge as they run the program repeatedly (Resnick, 1994/1997, pp. 68–69). Another model designed by the Media Lab enables children visiting the Boston Computer Museum to create a virtual ecosystem. Children select a variety of fish to inhabit a virtual aquarium and then program into each species features such as swimming depth and natural predators. Students learn about the complexities of nature as they watch combinations of fish coexist in the "aquarium" projected onto an oversized computer screen. High-powered artificial intelligence software maintained in a single physical location may soon be distributed over the Internet for use by an unlimited number of children worldwide.

One of the most dramatic changes resulting from Internet technology is the creation of new learning spaces defined by common interests and shared information, rather than by physical location (Berners-Lee, 1996; Mitchell, 1995, p. 22). Traditionally, school has been a transport-based operation. Whether on foot or by bus, train, or automobile, students go to school to take advantage of learning resources not available to them at home. In contrast, the Internet presents possibilities for rich learning opportunities to be transported to the learner (Tiffin & Rajasingham, 1995, p. 75). As affordable bandwidth (the feature of telecommunications that controls the volume of information delivered per second) increases, information that appeals to multiple senses may be delivered directly to the learner at any place and at any time (p. 41). In less than a decade, the Internet has evolved from a still, text-based medium to one that allows for instantaneous exchange of interactive audio and video formats. Computer laboratories are currently experimenting with the possibility of conveying smells via computers. At the moment, a student studying whales online can listen to whale calls, watch whales swim, chart the population changes over time for various species, and email questions directly to expert marine biologists. Soon, the child may also be able to smell the ocean air, no matter how far inland the student lives.

Children growing up with Internet technology are no longer satisfied to be passive viewers of online documents; instead, they expect to *do* something each time they go on the Internet (Harel, 1999). For children immersed in the combination of rich content and human interaction possible on the Internet, online "work spaces" may replace traditional "workplaces," such as the classroom (Navikas, 1998). Learning groups are no longer restricted to the other children physically present in a single classroom or school; instead, Internet users engage in online learning communities in which common interest in a particular topic or problem is the overriding criterion for membership. These communities—which are limited neither by the time parameters of the established school day nor by the geographical location of group members—displace information as the greatest value of the Internet. What can be done online with the information takes precedence over the mere availability of information (Negroponte, 1995, p. 183).

Time and space structures that are so clear in school are redefined in online spaces. On the Internet, there is no longer a clear distinction between work and free time (Mitchell, 1995, p. 101). No school bell rings to signal that it is time to shift to a different discipline or that learning time has ended for the day. Instead, time is structured according to the extent of a student's interest in a particular topic. The need for co-learners to be in the same place at the same time is eliminated by asynchronous electronic communication.[1] Unlike a telephone or face-to-face meeting, which requires all involved participants to be present at the same time, each email message is preserved on a computer, called a server, until the intended recipient logs on to collect the message. In this way, students can engage in learning projects with peers in different time zones worldwide. Rapidly, students are coming to see learning as a 24-hour-a-day activity. This is evidenced by a new problem college professors teaching online courses encounter: students expect an immediate response to questions they pose via email to an instructor, whether the message is sent at 10:00 A.M. or at midnight.

Teachers who once felt the need to keep pace with *Sesame Street* in order to gain their students' attention now face a whole new challenge: how to teach children who are growing up with the Internet. The Internet does not replace either the teacher or the direct learning experiences that take place in classrooms; instead, this new technology enables teachers to combine a broad range of virtual experiences with the direct experiences already possible in classrooms (Tiffin & Rajasingham, 1995; Turkle, 1995, pp. 236–237). Teachers in classrooms wired for Internet access face new decisions about what is important for students to learn and how they should learn it. For these schools, the Internet represents an opportunity to shift away from traditional instruction, in which the teacher is responsible for ensuring that all students in the class move through a uniform set of skills and information at roughly the same pace. As an integrated communication and information technology, the Internet can be used to support constructivist learning, in which each learner uses the available evidence to formulate his or her own understanding of any given problem.

Many teachers—some with and others without the Internet—already use components of constructivist learning in their teaching strategies. Constructivist learning is characterized by the following essential elements (Honebein, 1996; Savery & Duffy, 1996):

- *Authentic problem solving:* learning is focused on problems that are derived from the student's own experience and that have high personal relevance for the student.

- *Collaboration:* students work with others who share their interest to develop solutions to the problem. Learning is a social process in which students are constantly testing their understanding for compatibility with that of others.

- *Active engagement:* learning occurs through hands-on activities, not through rote processes such as repetition and memorization. Students' projects have real-life implications beyond the classroom or course grade.

- *Multiple perspectives:* students rely on a variety of information resources, each presenting a different perspective on the problem. These may include professional experts on the topic, as well as more traditional print or multimedia materials.

- *Multiple modes of representation:* students use a variety of formats to demonstrate their newly developed understanding. If possible, students actually carry out their solution to the problem they addressed.

- *Reflection on the learning process:* consideration of what problem-solving strategies were effective and which were not is essential to the learning process. In other words, students learn about learning, as well as about the particular topic.

Teachers who recognize any of these strategies are likely to say, "Yes, I do those things already in my classroom. What is so new or different about this?"

Where constructivist learning departs from traditional classroom instruction is in the relationship between teacher, learner, and knowledge. For centuries, formal education has been modeled on the assumption that there is a certain body of knowledge that is important for all students to know. Historically, the teacher's role has been to pass on that knowledge to students, who in turn are passive recipients of that knowledge. At the heart of the constructivist approach is the understanding that there does *not* exist outside the individual learner's mind a set body of knowledge to be acquired. Instead, students construct knowledge as they struggle to solve problems drawn from their own experience. Learning is an active, social, and creative process, which students themselves must carry out (von Glaserfeld, 1996).

When a constructivist approach is taken in a classroom, the teacher relinquishes center stage to the students. The learner, not the teacher, identifies both the problem to be solved and the steps by which it will be solved (Perkins, 1992, p. 52). In other words, the learner, not a textbook editor or curriculum designer, owns the problem and develops the strategies to solve it. The student is given far greater responsibility for learning and is accountable for the decisions he or she makes. When students select their own research topics, for example, students can no longer place blame on a teacher for assigning a "boring" project.

The teacher's responsibility shifts away from transmission of knowledge. Learning becomes "messy," as the teacher no longer leads all students through a set body of material at roughly the same pace. Instead, the teacher follows each student's lead and assumes the position of consultant and coach. The teacher's role is one of helping students to identify, articulate, and focus a problem; neither teacher nor textbook supplies the problem. The teacher challenges the learner's thinking constantly by asking questions, such as "Why?" and "What do you mean?" (Savery & Duffy, 1996, p. 145). Another critical task of the teacher's role in a constructivist approach is to create a learning environment that supports students' construction of knowledge. The learning environment must be rich in the information resources students need to examine a variety of perspectives on a wide range of topics. In addition, classroom communication patterns should support collaboration among students. Most important, the classroom must be closely and consistently connected to the students' real world, so that learning has a high degree of relevance. In other words, the classroom environment must be such that students can see the connection between their work in school and the world as they know it beyond the schoolyard fence.

The Internet as a technology has inherent features that support constructivist learning. The information resources currently available on the Internet expand the range of problems a teacher can expect a student to solve. In the past, student projects tended to be limited to the range of topics included in school library books and encyclopedia collections. A student who could not find enough material on a particular subject would abandon this research interest and select another topic to fit the resources immediately available. In contrast, the Internet provides a convenient, cost-effective means for students and their teachers to gather information on almost any topic that sparks a child's curiosity. If a child has just received a pet lizard as a birthday gift, it does not matter if the school's most closely related book is on alligators; the student can use the Internet to learn more about the new pet. The collective imagination of the teacher and students, not the scope of print resources in the classroom and school library, sets the limits for discovery.

Online, students can gather information from diverse perspectives and in a variety of multimedia formats. Students researching a controversial environmental issue, for example, can use the Web to read newspaper articles written from the perspectives of the various factions involved. Radio station Web sites may include interviews with the key leaders involved. As students listen to these interviews, they get a more accurate representation of the interview than they might from a written transcript. Maps projecting the environmental impact of various uses of the disputed land areas may also be accessible online. Learners, in turn, can use the same types of multimedia tools to present their understanding of the problem and the best possible solution they have derived from the information available.

When Internet use moves from a peripheral, or "add-on," status to a central role in student learning, the technology use provides a strong connection between the classroom and the world in which students will soon take their adult places. This "network of networks" enables learners to stay informed on current events, collaborate with peers across international lines, and consult with professional experts in almost every discipline. Without ever leaving the classroom, students can engage in group projects with other students worldwide. Common interest, rather than assignment to a particular class or neighborhood school, becomes the primary criteria for membership in a particular learning group. Constantly updated online news reports allow students to follow events in international relations, local politics, popular entertainment, professional sports, or almost any other area of interest. Global news reports, in particular, take on new meaning for students who communicate regularly with other teens worldwide. How is an American teen's perspective affected, for example, when the student has online friends who live in a country that has just suffered a natural disaster or is under surveillance by United States military forces?

The original purpose of the Internet was to advance scientific research by promoting collaboration among research institutions throughout the United States (Hafner & Lyon, 1996). Online, students may participate in discussion groups on almost any special interest. Students do not need special credentials to engage in these discussions; most often, the prerequisite for participation is interest in the topic. Using email to contact specialists in fields ranging from oceanography to modern art, students may network with these experts in much the same way that adult researchers do. When students go online regularly, learning need no longer be limited by the knowledge base of a single classroom teacher. Instead, the teacher becomes one of many experts available to students.

Web sites may be used to provide students with an audience for their schoolwork. Each site may be designed by a student or group of students to represent what they have learned about a particular topic. On the Internet, students can even build a site in collaboration with other students physically situated in remote locations. Classroom projects take on a very different meaning for students when, instead of being seen only by the teacher who grades the assignment, the project is posted on a Web site for anyone in the world to view. Using relatively simple Web site design, students can build in the capacity for anyone who views the site to email feedback to the student designers. The site can be revised as a student's understanding of the problem continues to develop beyond the arbitrary due date for the project.

Contrary to rhetoric used by advocates of digital technology, the Internet itself will not inherently drive or cause change in school learning. A technological innovation is shaped by the social context into which it is introduced—in this case, the classroom. In contrast to the instructional mode that dominated classroom learning throughout the 20th century, constructivist learning appears messy. Classroom learning ceases to be predictable as students work on a variety of topics, some of which may never even have occurred to the teacher. The pace of learning is variable; a time line dictated by the depth of a student's interest in a research problem may not coincide with the school's daily schedule or quarterly grading periods. Classroom communication patterns change dramatically as students use the Internet to work with online learning partners outside the teacher's jurisdiction and engage in conversations that are no longer centered in the classroom.

As disconcerting as this scenario may be to many teachers, it does reflect the world in which today's students are growing up. As schools acquire Internet access, teachers face the challenge of using this new technology in a way that is relevant to their cyber-savvy students' understanding of the world outside school. The question that remains is whether educators will follow in the footsteps of the earliest ARPANET (as the Internet was first named) users and employ the Internet for collaborative discovery processes or will appropriate this technology to support continued information delivery as the primary mode of classroom learning.

Notes

1. Synchronous communication requires the presence of all parties at the same time; in asynchronous communication, each participant's messages may be conveyed at any time. For example, a telephone conversation is synchronous, but email is asynchronous.

3

PATTERNS OF RESPONSE TO INNOVATION

SCHOOLS AND TECHNOLOGY

Last year when we got these computers which are very fast computers and open access to the Internet . . . I felt like the way people were talking about it . . . the way people were hyping this stuff up . . . they were talking about it as if this is going to radically change the way you teach and this is going to open up huge things and I guess I feel like [pause] it's just another piece . . . it definitely helps open up the avenue, especially for student choice in research projects but I don't know if it radically changes the way the classroom is structured and part of me thinks, well, of course not, because every time there is an idea like that which is just going to sort of change everything, it ends up being just another piece. . . . I see the computer as being a part of what we do but it doesn't change drastically the way we approach things.

—Teacher

The allure of computer technology is hard for educators to resist. Everywhere, advertisements for computers and Internet-related services promise an enhanced lifestyle to prospective users. Marketing aimed at educators assures them that this new technology will provide greater efficiency in classroom management, access to limitless information resources, and a magical appeal to maintain students' attention. Vendors play on teachers' fears by projecting that the teacher who fails to keep pace with the very latest developments in technology will soon fall further and further behind students. Keeping up seems nearly impossible, as new computer models and Internet services are announced almost daily. Frequently, school computer purchases are delayed by the notion that the new equipment will be obsolete before it is even unpacked from its shipping container. In this climate, it is very easy to become so focused on the newness of the particular technology that the critical lessons that can be learned by looking back at school use of earlier technologies are overlooked.

Historically, schools have been highly resistant to new technology. Deep in the closets of many classrooms are old movie projectors, filmstrip viewers, tape recorders, and other devices. Each of these machines was once hailed as a great asset to teachers, but it failed to transform classroom learning. Typically, the new device held special status due to its initial expense and novelty appeal. Use of the technology was reserved for special occasions and played a peripheral role in classroom learning. Very few of the new technologies introduced into classrooms ever became an integral part of day-to-day classroom routines. Most often, these new devices fell into disuse and eventually took their place in an audiovisual graveyard at the back of a school closet. Teachers frustrated by obstacles such as poor maintenance and inadequate software (e.g. filmstrips and audiotapes) continued to run their classrooms as they had prior to the purchase of the technology.

The fact that this equipment is not discarded but, instead, remains stored in schools' audiovisual closets for years is a reminder of the challenges schools face in acquiring new technology. Each piece of equipment was once considered a technical marvel essential to student learning and hence worthy of the high price tag. As overwhelming as the acquisition of the technology may be for schools on tight budgets, the purchase and installation of any new technology are only the first—and often the least complex—steps toward school technology use. The far greater challenge is to integrate the technology into classroom teaching and learning to an extent that justifies its expense.

The integration of computer technology into school curricula is problematic. Every teacher who has even contemplated using the Internet in the classroom is aware of the initial obstacles. For many schools, the expense of the hardware, software, and network wiring is prohibitive. In older school buildings, the installation of this equipment may reveal yet another problem: upgrading a dated electrical system that is inadequate to support new computers can be far more costly than the computer network itself. Added to the initial capital outlay are the monthly Internet and telephone service fees required for telecommunications use. Once the equipment is in place, not only are teachers expected to learn basic computer skills on their own; most often, they must also serve as technical experts in the absence of on-site technical staff to maintain the computer equipment. Given these challenges, it is not surprising that teachers have been slow to incorporate new technology into their practice. But how does technology use fit into classroom teaching and learning when these logistical obstacles are eliminated or minimized?

A look back in time suggests that there are other subtle, complex factors that may impede school technology use. Since the mid-19th century, increasingly sophisticated technologies ranging from the blackboard to the microcomputer have been tailored to and then imposed on the classroom. Historically, teachers have embraced only the technologies that have assisted them in accomplishing the priorities they maintain in the context of their daily classroom realities (Cuban, 1986, p. 65). Despite the variety of new technologies that have transformed daily life outside schools in recent decades, the day-to-day routines inside schools have remained relatively constant. An adult returning to school and assuming the role of student after many years away from the classroom would have very little difficulty knowing what to do. It is not enough to understand an innovation and its potential for learning; advocates of school technology use must recognize and account for how students and teachers operate on a day-to-day basis in classrooms.

The introduction of computer technology into the classroom raises fundamental questions about the traditional framework for learning on which schools are founded. The expectations of both teachers and students typically are shaped by the recitation model, which assumes a set body of knowledge to be transmitted from teacher to student (Wiske & Houde, 1988, pp. 209, 213). The day-to-day routines, rules, and relationships that make up the very fabric of a school have evolved over time to support the efficient delivery of information from teacher to student. A textbook, for example, streamlines the teacher's planning work load by providing a preselected set of concepts and facts to be presented to students. The teacher then is relieved of the arduous task of deciding which information and skills in social studies or mathematics are most important for students to learn in the limited time available. In theory, the use of a single set of textbooks across an entire school district ensures that each subsequent grade's teacher can assume that all students in the class have mastered a uniform body of knowledge in prior years.

The influence of this model extends beyond the classroom and is reflected in the very way schools are structured. The daily schedule, which allocates a set amount of time to the study of each discipline, provides all students with uniform exposure to each discipline. The passage of students from grade to grade at the conclusion of the school year is based on the expectation that the teacher moves all students at approximately the same pace through a set of designated material in each discipline. Standardized testing, which places priority on a certain set of skills and facts, assumes uniformity in learning nationwide and serves as a point of comparison believed to be more reliable than the grades assigned by individual teachers across a variety of school settings. These are only a few of the practices—each of which emphasizes efficiency of scale rather than attention to the individual learner—that continually help to reinforce the underlying belief that the purpose of school is for students to acquire a set body of knowledge. Inherent in each of these practices is the understanding that the teacher—as deliverer of information—is in control of the direction, pace, and scope of student learning. It is within this model that teachers and students take their places and assume their respective roles within the school.

The more creative the technology use, the greater the extent to which these established school practices may be disrupted. What schools are for, what should be taught, and how children learn are all unavoidable questions when schools experiment with the new technology (Cuban, 1986, p. 84; Papert, 1996, pp. 191–192). If used in a way that is central to classroom learning, computer technology creates new tensions, rooted in issues far more complex than the cost of hardware and software. The relative emphasis on learning content versus learning process is called into question. With the vast amount of information instantly available to students, for example, is it more important for a student to recite a series of historical facts at the time of a class test or to be able to locate and use the same facts at the time of actual need? The emphasis that schools have long placed on individual achievement is challenged, as technology use facilitates collaboration. How does a teacher assess and report on the collective knowledge of a group of students as compared with what individual students can do on their own? Who controls the pace and direction of learning when convenient access to vast information resources displaces that which the textbook once held forth as most important to learn? Teachers', parents', and students' beliefs about what constitutes a "real school" are challenged by any fundamental change in these and other established school practices (Tyack & Tobin, 1994, p. 466).

The potential for computer technology to transform learning challenges the traditional relationship among the teacher, the student, and knowledge. As a result of new technology, the amount of information available to teachers and students has increased exponentially. The weblike learning approach enabled by hyper-linked documents displaces the sequential learning that, in the past, has lent efficiency to school curricula. For the most part, learners in earlier days all had access to the same finite amount of information, along with adequate time to process it. The understanding was that there existed only one rational conclusion or correct answer to any given problem (Bailey, 1996, p. 173). Now each learner may use powerful Internet search engines and hyper-links to gather a unique combination of information on any given topic. The assumption that the teacher is responsible for delivering a set body of knowledge to students is undermined as technology affords students easy access to unlimited information resources and direct communication with experts in any discipline.

The introduction of any new technology into the classroom tests the relative value of different types of knowledge. Over a century ago, American teachers struggled to keep pace with the demands placed on schools by business leaders in need of a workforce armed with skills that

matched the needs of the emerging industrial economy. Nineteenth-century teachers struggled to fit technical drawing skills that not all educators considered worthy of school time into an already "overcrowded curriculum" (Stevens, 1995, pp. 38–39). Likewise, today's teachers must decide where computer skills fit in with the myriad of demands made on public schools. As students work with powerful new multimedia tools, for example, visual information skills take on new importance. In addition to being able to read and write, students growing up in the Internet Age must be able to interpret and in turn create electronic documents that wed text with highly sophisticated visual images. Most often, decisions related to the allocation of limited classroom time are influenced by a wide variety of factors far beyond the teacher's control. In the case of the programming language Logo, American teachers were forced to eliminate it from high school instruction in favor of Pascal, when the latter was adopted as the uniform testing standard by the Advanced Placement Exams (Aglianos, 1996, p. 17).

The overcrowded curriculum becomes even more problematic when one considers that there are no clear boundaries to the open-ended, constructivist learning made possible by the Internet. Everything about the school setting—from the standard class size to the time allocated for specific tasks—stems from the 20th-century emphasis on efficiency and standardization in public education. Papert's vision of student learning exploding with rich connections across many domains of knowledge is in direct conflict with the teacher's need to maintain uniformity of outputs, as defined by the material students cover each term (Agalianos, 1996; Papert, 1993, p. 103). In England and Wales, Logo was added to the National Curriculum, but it still did not fit into the school day. Teachers felt pressured to ensure student success on standardized national exams and had little time to devote to the open-ended learning process for which Logo was designed. The end result was that Logo use was relegated to a three-week instructional unit at the periphery of the curriculum (Agalianos, 1997).

When learners use telecommunications technology to move beyond time and space boundaries, the concept of school as a physically defined community is blurred. Schools exist as physical places solely to bring teachers and students together (Mitchell, 1995, p. 67). There is nothing inherent in learning itself that requires a school building or classroom. The prototypical school building is designed for optimal control of students. Classrooms and corridors are designed to allow for constant surveillance. Students have no space to call their own, other than cramped lockers, which may be subject to search by school officials (Sitton, 1980). Once a student logs onto the Internet, the classroom walls dissolve as boundaries for learning. Students can use hyper-links to pursue a particular topic of interest well beyond the confines of the school curriculum. Anyone, anywhere becomes a potential learning partner. Teacher control over student learning becomes elusive, as each student may be in a different online space at any given time. Students growing up with computers may keep one step ahead of school attempts to control student Internet use. For example, most American schools with Internet access do not provide email accounts to students. Since the introduction of commercial Web sites offering free email accounts, however, students have used school computers to access these sites and set up and use their own email accounts. When these sites were first introduced, many teachers were not even aware of Web-based email, much less of the fact that students were using it in the classroom to send and receive email.

In contrast to the rhetoric used by advocates of computer technology, the technology itself does not inherently change classroom teaching and learning. These changes are unlikely to be anticipated and accounted for in school technology plans. It is far easier to plan for the obvious capital expense and physical renovations required for Internet use than it is to foresee the more subtle challenges to core assumptions about how schools operate. Typically, the first application of technology is to do better than that which is already being done (Papert, 1993, pp. 184–185). During the 1980s, the microcomputer earned the reputation as a very expensive workbook, when rote grammar and computational exercises were transferred from paper workbook to computer screen. More recently, many college professors have used course Web sites by simply transferring quizzes and grading to these sites, rather than experimenting with the new possibilities for learning presented by interactive online technology. Electronic classrooms that feature computerized white boards for display and storage of information presented in class lectures tend to be used to enhance rather than change an instructional model in which the teacher delivers information to students.

Initially, school technology use fits into the preexisting routines teachers have developed over time to cope with "classroom press"—that is, the combination of pressures that causes teachers to become isolated, exhausted, and focused on immediate needs (Huberman, 1983; Kerr, 1991, p. 120; Olson, 1988). Many teachers, for example, are not using email for global communication; they value email most as a convenient means of communication with the teacher down the hall. Over time, teachers may modify their practice as they discover new ways of learning made possible by the technology. The result is an interactive relationship in which the school setting shapes the way the technology is used at the same time that technology use may lead to change in the school (Schofield, 1996). The same teachers who first use email to communicate with each other might discover over time, for instance, that as the technology facilitates team planning they can engage their students in more interdisciplinary learning.

The relationship between teachers' pedagogical beliefs and their classroom technology use is not clear. In some cases, the introduction of new technology into the classroom reinforces existing classroom practices. The practice of confining students to a limited number of pre-selected Web sites rather than teaching students effective searching strategies restricts student access to information in the same way that reliance on a textbook does. Still, the innovation may eventually challenge existing classroom practice and become a catalyst for change (Zhao, 1998, p. 310). If a student use the links available on the teacher-selected sites, the student can pursue the topic at hand well beyond the scope of a textbook or the set of Web sites the teacher had originally intended for student use.

In either case, change tends to be slow. When technology is introduced as a means of promoting constructivist pedagogy, teachers do not automatically abandon the habits associated with the recitation model, even if they have accepted in theory the new pedagogical approach. As with any other school change effort, teachers do not instantly change their practice. Teachers encounter a number of unanticipated conflicts with their long-established day-to-day routines as they make the the the leap from theory to practice (Wiske & Houde, 1988, p. 209). A teacher may accept the constructivist tenet that students are most likely to learn when they pursue topics of their own interest and yet have difficulty relinquishing control over the direction of student learning. This is not to say that computer technology has no potential role as catalyst for school change. Given adequate time and support from expert advisors, teachers may examine and resolve conflicts between their preexisting classroom practice and the constructivist pedagogy afforded by computer technology (p. 214).

Some teachers do believe that their role has changed as a result of using computers in their classrooms. But the connection between the introduction of technology and any perceived shift in the relationship among the teacher, the student, and knowledge remains unclear. These teachers use terms such as *facilitator* and *coach* to describe their new role. They report less time spent lecturing and more time spent with individual students as technology is used in the classroom. The teachers believe that using computer technology results in a fundamental redistribution of power and authority in their classrooms. According to these teachers, students begin to recognize over time that the teacher does not know everything. With continued computer use, students come to view the teacher as a colearner (Kerr, 1991, p. 127). But not all educators view the changes that may accompany classroom computer use as positive. After France implemented a nationwide program to equip schools with computers and to provide teachers with basic computer skills, the teachers complained that they could not conduct whole-class instruction without a one to one student to computer ratio (Vickers & Smalley, 1995, p. 272).

Technology alone will not bring about fundamental change in classroom teaching and learning. To date, schools have placed a disproportionate emphasis on the information functions of the new technologies—that is, the functions that align most closely with the transmission of knowledge from teacher to students (Jerald, 1998b, p. 111; Papert, 1998). The Internet is no exception; in the classroom, it is viewed more as a source of information than as a communication tool. Students are much more likely to be found searching the Web for project information than emailing or using chat rooms from a classroom computer. The number of American schools with Internet access has increased steadily, so that in 1998 eighty-five percent of schools in the United States reported having Internet access. The percentage of Internet-using schools providing students with email access, however, dropped from 43% in 1994 to 39% in 1997 (Jerald, 1998a, pp. 102–103).

Another question is whether the new technology has the inherent ability to foster teacher change, or is new technology most likely to be used by teachers who are already innovative in their professional practice? A study of nine exemplary technology-using schools revealed that students are most likely to use computer technology to support constructivist learning in schools that already emphasize student-centered, project-based learning prior to the introduction of computers (Means & Olson, 1995, p. 160). Similarly, critical characteristics were shared by the six teachers involved in a transcontinental, Internet-based writing project that brought together students from six diverse North American schools. In their practice, these teachers emphasized learning focused on student interests. They viewed technology use as a means of accomplishing other learning goals, rather than as an end unto itself. And each of the six teachers was constantly seeking new ways to improve student learning (Garner & Gillingham, 1996, p. 135).

The most innovative computer uses tend not to be systematic; they are the result of pioneering teachers working alone or in small groups (Garner & Gillingham, 1996, p. 12; Papert, 1993, pp. 38–39). In order to provide students with computer-based learning opportunities, these technology leaders put forth extraordinary effort above and beyond what is reasonable to expect of teachers. These teachers most often act as both curriculum expert and technician responsible for maintaining the computer hardware and software. It is not unusual to find the responsibility for maintaining a school's network falling on the teacher with the most sophisticated computer knowledge, even though that teacher already has a full day in the classroom. These technology leaders learn the necessary skills on their own time, often depending on friends and relatives employed in computer-related fields for assistance. Classroom computer use may represent a drain on the teacher's personal finances, as the teacher sooner or later faces the choice of purchasing equipment and supplies for the classroom or stopping short of maximizing students' computer learning experiences. One high school teacher, for example, became so frustrated with her students' lack of access to a printer that she purchased a printer along with a year's supply of paper and ink cartridges for her classes.

In response to public pressure for schools to incorporate computer use into student learning, school administrators often point to the technology use of an exemplary teacher as evidence that the school is keeping pace with new technology. Unfortunately, these efforts fall far short of reaching all students. In my own search for a school in which to study students' Internet use, I discovered school after school in which extensive Internet experience was gained only by the small number of students assigned to an innovative teacher. The remainder of the students in these schools had little or no in-school exposure to the Internet. Also, these pioneering teachers sooner or later encounter institutional obstacles to their innovative technology use. For example, an individual teacher has little capacity to revise a school schedule consisting of 50-minute class periods to gain the larger time blocks necessary for students to create their own Web pages. Research across four nations—France, Norway, Scotland, and Australia—indicates that the most successful technology integration during the 1980s resulted from a systemic approach, coupled with the active involvement of teachers in the planning process (Vickers & Smalley, 1995).

Even with institutional support, teachers alone cannot change the way students learn in school. If the instructional model shifts from content delivery to student inquiry, there are many accommodations that teachers themselves must make. Students can take responsibility for their own learning only when the teacher is willing to share control over the learning process with students. If student interests are honored in the selection of classroom projects, the teacher may become immersed in unfamiliar topics. The teacher is no longer in a position to deliver information to students and, instead, guides students through the process of researching the problem themselves. At times, the student may know more about a particular topic than does the teacher. The teacher's authority is no longer grounded in the information that the educator has to impart to students; instead, the teacher becomes a colearner with students and, in doing so, provides students with a role model for effective learning. But these changes in the teacher's role imply a corresponding change in the student's role. What is not accounted for in initiatives aimed at fundamental school change is how students must adapt to the new teaching and learning environment of the classroom. What are the corresponding changes in the student's role, and are students ready to make these changes?

The recitation model, which rests on the assumption that it is the teacher's responsibility to deliver a set body of knowledge to students, has also shaped the student's role. Students' lives in the classroom are governed by the notion that "teacher knows best" (Sarason, 1996, p. 217). In school, students learn quickly that teachers talk and students listen (Aspy, 1986, p. 57). Students learn to look for the "right" answers to teachers' questions, even though the reality of the information age is that there is not a single right answer to any given problem (pp. 24–25). Few teachers attempt to explain the complex, abstract concepts behind the information students are expected to master. Given the amount of material teachers must cover in a relatively short period of time, there is inadequate time for anything but the most superficial treatment of each topic. The student is unable to see any logical connection between daily lessons or between classroom learning and the far more complex world outside school (Sizer, 1984).

From the outset of their formal education, students learn to respond to classroom instruction with passivity (Goodlad, 1984, p. 233). They quickly come to understand that their duty in school is to accept without question the information passed on to them (Sizer, 1984, p. 92). By third grade, students have learned to "go along" with the teacher and have settled into the passive learner role (Aspy, 1986, p. 49). It takes very little time for children to learn that, in school, they are to follow the teacher's directions, whether they are to stand in a straight line, raise one's hand to speak, or color within the lines. Playfulness and creativity are abandoned at the classroom door in favor of conformity and passivity.

As older students move through secondary school, they experience increased teacher control. Any personal connections that students may have felt with their elementary school teachers are replaced by countless rules. The school day becomes far more structured, with a set amount of time allocated for each subject of study. Standardized tests loom ahead as key determinants in students' future educational and career paths. As teachers lead students through the curriculum, there is little time for students' curiosity or for connections between disciplines.

Students learn that there is minimal benefit in raising questions or exploring problems that extend beyond the material immediately at hand (Sizer, 1984, pp. 54–55).

This is not to say that the student is powerless in the classroom. The teacher-student relationship requires students' complicity. Students can choose not to go along with the social organization and processes of the school. Schools are highly dependent on students' consistent voluntary conformity to the passive role they learned from their earliest days in the classroom. Students disproportionately outnumber teachers and administrators. Collectively, the students have the power to challenge classroom and school practices and procedures, but they rarely do so (Sizer, 1984).

The 1999 fatal ambush of Colorado's Columbine High School is an extreme and tragic example of two students opting not to conform with the learned expectations for participation in school. But even the slightest student deviation from compliance with the teacher's expectations stands out as an unusual occurrence in school. Students learn quickly that even speaking out of turn or arriving a few minutes late for class may be considered a serious enough offense to warrant punishment. At a time when adolescents should be taking more control of their own learning, most students tend to put their minds "on hold" as the primary alternative. From the start of their schooling, students have learned that this is the necessary trade-off to participate in the setting where their friends are (Goodlad, 1984, p. 233). Just as previous technology-based reforms failed to account for the underlying assumption that the teacher's role is to maintain order and deliver the curriculum, current efforts fail to address explicitly the habitual passivity that marks the student's role in the recitation model.

Outside school, children are anything but passive in their computer-based learning. In contrast to their teachers' understanding of the Internet as an information-delivery system, children use the technology as an integrated communication and information system. "N-geners," children growing up with Internet access, use the technology to support constructivist learning (Tapscott, 1998). There are countless Web sites, for example, that children and teens have conceived and constructed as forums in which to share their own artwork and literature relating to highly specialized topics. The young participants in these online spaces are highly critical of and expect continual improvement in each other's work. Seymour Papert, a preeminent thinker on children's computer use, has predicted that eventually children's and teens' out-of-school technology use will serve as a catalyst for fundamental change in schools (Papert, 1996, p. 15). "Kid power," the name he gives to the influence of students' going into school having used a full range of computer technology functions at home, may pressure schools to shift from the recitation model to teaching practices based on constructivist pedagogy (Papert, 1998).

At the moment, however, there is very little information available on what occurs when students enter the classroom as fluent Internet users. Research on classroom technology use tends to focus on the teacher's perspective. Garner and Gillingham, for example, describe themselves as "sympathetic witnesses" to teachers using the Internet for an online student writing project (1996, p. 5). Countless surveys have questioned teachers regarding their classroom technology use, but few researchers ask students directly how often and for what purposes they use computers in school. Studies that account for children's perspectives on network technology use typically occur outside schools or in settings where researchers have intervened to create a lab in a classroom. Intervention by a research agency may take the form of supplementing the hardware and software available in the classroom, supplying computer-based curricula, and/or providing professional development and technical support for teachers. In any case, the combination of resources provided by researchers may be driven by an agenda different from that of the school. The potential outcome is that the relationship between preexisting classroom routines and the new technology becomes less clear. These studies provide valuable information on the potential for school computer use, but they still fall short of providing a valid account of how students use the Internet when the school adopts the innovation to meet its own purposes. The result is that the obstacles teachers face when they try to integrate technology use into their practice are well documented, but far less is known about students' experiences as classroom computer users.

During the spring of 1998, I had the opportunity to learn from 34 Cityview School students how they use the Internet. These 12- and 13- year-old teens are part of the first generation of students born since the widespread dissemination of the microcomputer in 1983–84. Even though only 11 of these students have computers at home, most of them have some access to the Internet outside school. They all encounter computers in a variety of settings in their daily lives and, unlike the adults around them, do not know a way of life without computers. Computer use is a high priority at their school. In contrast to settings in which the technology was introduced for university research purposes, Cityview School administrators and teachers initiated a technology plan for their own purposes and acquired adequate computer hardware, software, technical support, and professional development to support classroom Internet use. I was most interested in how students growing up in the Internet Age use the Internet in school, an institution defined by roles and relationships established long before the development of computer technology. It was easy enough to observe students as they worked at computer terminals in the classroom, but what I really wanted was to be able to see past the computer monitors to understand what these teens were doing once connected to the Internet. In other words, I was looking for a window into their online lives.

4

ONLINE AND OFFLINE

IT'S ALL REAL

Mainly what I've been doing with them is to go through the basics of the computer system. What RAM means, what a hard drive does, where it's located. The basics of a computer system, the desktop, the menus.

—Teacher

. . . I got a computer at my house now. And now it's like . . . I don't know all the two thousand "QP" whatever. I don't even know what it is, you know. But it's a good computer, and basically all you want is a computer that's not going to bother you with technical things. . . . You know, I'm not picky about what programs it has and how pretty it looks; I just want it to do whatever I need it to do, you know.

—Student

Since the invention of the radio, children and teens have gathered at the house of the friend with the best home entertainment appliances. Just as their parents and grandparents once huddled around a radio or television, today's adolescents are quick to discover who among them has the fastest, most powerful computer. In 1996, my own kitchen instantly turned into a teen cyber-café of sorts when my 12-year-old twin daughters were given their own computer. With no other space available in our small home, the computer was squeezed into a corner between the microwave and refrigerator. The more I listened from my desk in the next room as my daughters and their friends logged onto the Internet each afternoon, the less I understood what they were doing. I had been using the Internet for two years by that time, but the adolescents gathered in my kitchen seemed to be experiencing this technology in a way that I did not fully comprehend.

Before long, I became convinced that the many teens I encountered in my professional and personal life were doing something very new and different with computer technology. Certainly, each generation of teens throughout the 20th century had more technologically advanced playthings than their parents. But what I was witnessing seemed to be more significant than the differences between a phonograph and compact disc player. Internet technology appeared to be offering teens a whole new set of possibilities that had not existed at all for the adults around them. But what exactly were those possibilities? What did these teens do once the computer had completed that string of noises and signals to indicate they had established a connection? What was it they were connecting to? Initially, I viewed language as a possible key to discovering answers to this question. What could we learn about what the Net generation does online from the words and phrases middle school students employ to describe their Internet use?

For six months, I listened closely to Cityview School students talk about how they use the Internet. In the many hours I spent with these students, the only special lexicon they employed to describe their Internet use pertained to the procedures they used to log on to the Internet or to gain access to individual Internet sites. Students use a variety of generic technical terms to describe the specific type, reliability, and ease of use of the computer hardware, software, and services associated with Internet use. Examples of these terms include *email, links, log on,* and *download.* In addition, students adapt commercial labels for Internet-related products and their features. For example, students *IM* each other using the "instant message" feature offered by a major Internet service provider. Once they are logged on to the Internet, students use location metaphors to describe their movement between different sites. These words and phrases conventionally describe movement between physical places. Students use *going to, leaving, getting lost,* and other similar expressions to describe their movement from one Web site to another, even though the teens never physically leave their computer terminals.

All of these terms relate specifically to the technical aspects of gaining access to the online spaces formed by the Internet, not to what the students do in these spaces. What caught my attention as students talked about their Internet use was the conspicuous absence of any special lexicon to describe what they do once online. When students talk about how they use this technology, the more experienced Internet users do not distinguish between their online and offline activities and relationships. It is difficult to determine when these students are talking about online friends as opposed to friends with whom their primary contact occurs in traditional physical settings, such as school and neighborhood.

In my conversations with Mark, for example, I frequently had to ask for clarification of what occurred on the Internet. Mark is a fluent Internet user and is recognized by his classmates and online friends as a technical expert. His description of his encounters with an online friend sounds like a meeting in the school cafeteria or corridor: "Um, I think once in a while, I—when he, when he sees me, he says, 'I got this new—there's a cool site,' or something and so I just go to the site and see." The friend never "saw" Mark on the Internet. Instead, he detected through the synchronous email function instant messaging that Mark was also logged on to the Internet. The friend then commenced communication with Mark. In turn, Mark's reaction of going to "see" the site his friend suggested did not involve any physical movement beyond a few keystrokes and clicks of the mouse. Mark did not walk down the street to "go to the site and see." If his description were removed from the context of an interview about his Internet use, Mark's response easily could have described a visit to a local comic book store or music outlet recommended by a friend.

My experience with the most fluent Internet users among the Cityview girls was similar. In addition to using the Internet for assignments in their classroom, Carla, Sarah, and Lynn all have had periods of home Internet access. Carla uses the Internet frequently at home. At one point, her home access was discontinued for a month after her parents became worried by her older sister's constant—"24-7" (24 hours a day, 7 days a week), in Carla's words—Internet use. Lynn has home Internet service. She feels pressured by her parents to limit her use to homework, but she still finds time to go online for other purposes. Sarah had spent much of her after-school time at home, vying with her brother for online time, until her family's service was interrupted indefinitely by technical problems with her home computer.

When Sarah and Carla speculated about whether or not it was "safe" to purchase merchandise through the Web, Lynn responded:

> It depends on the company . . . like if it's a huge company, like, like, something like—you would trust, but if it was something little, like I went to this Web site once, I didn't know what I was going to—but it was like a costume renting place that, I don't know—I was just—I didn't want to rent a costume or anything, but I just tried it out, but it was such a little company. . . .

As Lynn describes her online encounter with the costume shop, it is difficult for the listener not to imagine a teen visiting a small store in a nearby shopping mall. But Lynn never moved from her computer. The "shop," if it exists as a physical entity at all, may be no more than a warehouse for the costumes, rather than a storefront into which prospective customers walk to try on costumes. In her mind, Lynn had experienced enough of the shop to determine that she did not trust the business. She did not need physical dimensions for the shop or her visit to it be real to her. Students consistently describe their online relationships and activities this way, making no distinction in their language between their technology-mediated experiences on the Internet and activities and conversations that occur offline in the physically defined places, such as the school and homes, that make up their offline habitat.

Cityview students did not always provide enough contextual clues for me to determine whether they were describing experiences that occurred online or in more traditional settings. In early interviews, I used the terms *virtual* and *real* when I asked students to distinguish which of the events they were describing occurred on the Internet and which did not. On several occasions, students seemed not to understand my question. One day, I became confused as I tried to follow Mark's description of how he and his friends exchange computer files online. As Mark spoke, I was not able to tell which of his friends were classmates or neighbors and which were other teens he had met via the Internet. I asked Mark whether one friend he mentioned was an online friend or one he had met in "real life." Mark was too polite to state what was obvious to him, but the puzzled look on his face said it all. To these students, there was no real or virtual. Whereas the adults around them—myself included—distinguished between the real world in which we had grown up and the virtual world of the Internet, these students were moving very fluidly back and forth between physically defined spaces and online spaces. To them, it was all real.

When Cityview students go on the Internet, they leave their physical presence behind and enter into a meeting of the minds. Even though they have no physical presence in the spaces created on the Internet, the students "see" and "hear" each other as though they were engaged in face-to-face communication and interaction in the same room. As their minds meet through digital communication, the students engage in relationships and activities that are as real to them as anything they do in their physically defined habitats. In my subsequent conversations with students, I replaced *virtual* and *real* with the terms *online* and *offline* to indicate activities and relationships that are Internet-mediated and those that are not.

The students' access to these online spaces is dependent on computer technology. But the computer, network, and other technical components that combine to enable access to the Internet are of little interest to the students as they move between the online spaces and their offline habitat. Although Jeff is a fluent Internet user, he isn't even sure what kind of computer he has:

> . . . I don't know all the two thousand "QP" whatever. I don't even know what it is, you know. But it's a good computer, and

> basically all you want is a computer that's not going to bother you with technical things, so you can sort of do whatever you want and it's not going to take you an hour to do. You know, I'm not picky about what programs it has and how pretty it looks; I just want it to do whatever I need it to do, you know.

His assessment of the various Internet services he and his friends use is based on what each service enables them to do, not on specific technical features. Jeff explained why he and some of his Cityview classmates do not like using a major Internet service provider:

> It's really bad. It's slow, it's—like I don't know too much about the Internet and the way it works, but you're not allowed to play online games and it's, it's like impossible to get onto sometimes when you . . . really need to, like during prime time it's impossible to get on. . . .

Colin, another fluent Internet user, took an extracurricular course at another local school. He recounted in a monotone voice what he learned: "I attended a telecommunications on the Internet class and um, I did actually learn a little about how the signal goes through the hub to the different things, yeah." He then shifted the conversation to describe how he learned to use the Internet "just by having it, pretty much." By the end of the telecommunications course, Colin knew little more about how his computer and the Internet function technically than the typical eighth-grader knows about a refrigerator and the electrical system that powers it.

Kerri had just begun to use the Internet in school this year and did not yet have home access. She was the only student to talk about the technology itself in any detail. Two months after moving to a new home, her family's computer was still packed in boxes. According to Kerri, her mother had not yet contacted a computer technician to come set it up and refused to allow Kerri to put it together. A Cityview faculty professional day gave Kerri the opportunity to assemble the computer while her mother was away at work:

> I just took it out of the box, I started putting it together. And she [Kerri's mother] came home and she's like, "What are you

doing?" . . . [mimics mother's demanding tone]. "Nothing" [under her breath]. She's like, "Kerri, you really wanta put that computer together?" I'm like, "Yeah, Mom, I *really* want to put that computer together," and she was like, "Well, you know a little bit about computers—you've been around computers for five years. [momentary pause followed by change to a firm tone of voice mimicking mother] Nope! Enough." But there's like directions and pictures. I was like, "Mom, come on." So I saved my mom like $50.

Kerri's subsequent efforts to persuade her mother to extend the telephone cord to reach the computer revealed that Kerri's end goal was not the technical project of assembling the computer:

And like here's the computer back at the beginning of the house and like, the phone thing is like on the other side of the wall, but so, but there're doors here, so my mom has to run it around the whole room and then bring it in there. And I was like, "Mom, I can get Juno! That's free email! I can get it!"

Kerri was far more interested in what she could do with the computer once it was activated. The technical tasks were only the means to the end of gaining access to the Internet and, in particular, of being able to communicate through email.

The students' lack of interest in the computer technology itself is similar to the attitude most automobile drivers take toward their cars. The driver's primary concern is not how many cubic centimeters the engine is or how fast the pistons fire; what the driver wants to know is "Will the car get me to my destination on time?" Carla, who uses the Internet frequently both at home and school, makes a distinction between the technical and social aspects of using the Internet. ". . . I don't like the Net," she states but then clarifies, "But well, I like it . . . but it's computing and computers [that] confuse me." She loves to meet new friends (especially boys) in chat rooms and through instant messaging but has little interest in the computer itself.

In the case of the Internet, the computer and related telecommunications devices become the vehicle to transport students to online spaces of their choice. This is in sharp contrast to the concerns voiced by one of the Cityview teachers, who had designed and implemented a plan by which each student becomes "computer certified" when the student has learned ". . . the basics of the computer system." To become certified, a student must know

> . . . exactly what is happening on the access of the Internet: that they are accessing a terminal or a computer, that . . . the signal out of the computer is going to a hub, the hub is going to [the] room over here where the modem is, and where there is a connect[ion] going outside to AT&T, to [the Internet service provider].

As planned by school personnel, students begin this learning process in fourth grade and, at each successive grade level, develop an increasingly sophisticated understanding of how the technology works.

The invention of the automobile and the subsequent development of an interstate highway system expanded expectations for physical travel. As automobile travel became reasonably reliable and affordable, it became possible for Americans to engage in relationships and activities beyond the distance a human could conveniently travel on foot or by horse-drawn carriage. Railroad service allowed humans to travel greater distances but locked passengers into scheduled times and stops. Each automobile driver controlled his or her own departure and arrival times and could travel to any location on the rapidly growing network of roads. Students growing up with microcomputers and the Internet assume that their minds can travel instantly to destinations far beyond the boundaries set by their physical surroundings. The automobile and highway system made possible new spaces in the American landscape, ranging from suburban housing to drive-through banks. Similarly, the Internet has led to the access and availability of expansive spaces for the mind, ranging from chat rooms to Web rings. For the students, the computer and telecommunications that constitute the Internet are merely the vehicle and highway system needed to reach these new spaces.

Unlike the suburban landscape that grew up out of the widespread dissemination of automobile technology, the spaces made possible by the computer and Internet have no conventional physical dimensions.

The Internet as used by Cityview students consists of many constantly changing spaces. Each space is defined by the communication of its inhabitants. A chat room, for example, is only a technical possibility until at least two persons enter it and engage in conversation with each other. The conversation—not traditional physical boundaries, such as walls and ceiling—shapes the "room."

When students use the Internet, they become architects of these online spaces. Internet "game rooms," for example, are designed by the players. One of Jeff's favorite rainy-day activities is to invite friends over to his house to play online games. "It's like, it's, it's—it's a game," he says. "And basically you just play against other people. You go into different rooms and set up games and just play, and then you get ranks and—so, it's fun, you know." Jeff and his friends like best the war games available through one particular Internet service. Colin would rather participate in role-playing games:

> . . . [T]here are a lot of *good* people out there, and a lot of *great* kids, and you know, [the Internet's] a great recreational tool because I'm into role playing . . . and there are all of these RPG [role-playing game] rooms, where people who enjoy it just like I do go in and take on a character and just talk and act out a scene. . . . It's really cool.

Colin and Jeff do not go into physically defined rooms to play these games. They establish the dimensions of the online space through their negotiation of a set of game rules and the role(s) each player assumes. Unlike the fixed walls of a physical room, the boundaries of the online room fluctuate according to the exchange between players. The entry and exit of new players determine the size of the game room. The landscape of the RPG room Colin described is defined by the players to meet the needs of the characters in each scene acted out. The room is continually reshaped by the communication among players. If Jeff and his online friends cease to engage in "war" with each other, the room loses its shape as a battlefield.

When students use the Internet, their purpose for being online helps to shape the spaces. Students quickly move beyond the novelty effect of the technology to become self-directed in their Internet use. Jeff saw little point in logging on to the Internet without a specific purpose:

> . . . [I]t's really good, if you know what you're looking for. But if you don't know what you're looking for, you're gonna just, you're gonna be lost. . . . If you just . . . hop on the Internet with no idea what you're doing, cuz . . . you just want to be on the Internet—it's like, "Yeah, hello, I'm on the Internet." But it's better to know, to have a reason to be on the Internet, is what I think.

Knowing why they are using the Internet is essential to students' ability to navigate the Internet. Since the rooms do not exist as physical entities, they cannot be described by physical location and decor.

The critical dimension of each online space is the common interest of the inhabitants. Kristen, a newcomer to the Internet, described how each chat room is defined by the topic discussed:

> . . . [T]here are like different types of chat rooms, like there's Spice Girls [a popular music group] chat rooms and then there's chat rooms that are like, um, "what do you think about Einstein's e = mc squared . . . so you probably use the type that are intellectual for a project, and Spice Girls for . . . entertainment.

She explained how she chose which chat rooms to frequent:

> . . . [I]t's just that I go to topics that I like, so I can talk to other people that I like. I go . . . for that reason. And if it is a confusing and annoying chat room then I leave, and I wouldn't like that.

Given that the chat room has no physical dimensions, Kristen does not walk out of the room. A participant leaves the online space by disengaging from that particular conversation.

Although the Internet affords global communication, not every online space is public. Online, students are not identified by their physical characteristics. Only the person's mind is present on the Internet. Students can maintain multiple identities under different screen names, none of which needs to correspond with the student's offline identity. Colin described how he uses one of two screen names, depending on whether he wants to appear publicly or privately online:

> . . . I have one screen name which is Cal Zenkow, and uh people know me as Cal. . . . [N]o one knows my last name. I don't even want people to know I am Colin. You know, the most people know is that I am just from Riverview. . . . I had another screen name for a while, Mario IM. . . . [T]hat was when I first got onto the Internet. You know, I was like, "I can have another screen name. . . . I can take on an identity". . . . But once I got more experience on the Internet, the novelty sort of wore off . . . people know I'm really not Mario. So, I changed my name to Doctor Topper 36 and Doctor Topper is another character in one of the Mario games. It's very obscure. Only real Mario maniacs really know about it. . . . [T]he 36 is just a number. . . . [A]bout five people know that I'm both—Cal Zenkow and Doctor Topper. You know, only my closest friends. . . . Doctor Topper is a screen name I go to sometimes when I want to be left alone.

Through his choice of screen names, Colin controls the size of the online space in which he functions at any given time. The name "Cal Zenkow" exposes him to online interaction with a large number of other individuals. The second screen name, "Doctor Topper," allows him to maintain a private space accessible only to his five closest friends. Neither screen name has any connection to his offline identity.

On the Internet, Cityview students design the spaces in which they work and play. These spaces are defined by students' communication with other individuals with whom they share common interests. Internet technology provides the opportunity for students' minds to forge relationships and engage in a variety of collaborative activities, free of the limits traditionally imposed by physical space and time. The computer and related technical components of the Internet are of little interest to the students; their focus is on the activities and relationships possible once they are logged on to the Internet. Meanwhile, the adults around them for whom the technology is not yet transparent are left far behind.

5

FUN, BUT NOT ALL GAMES

LIVING AND LEARNING ONLINE

. . . I think the Web pages are good because . . . you get to—
when you start designing it and doing all those kinds of crazy
decorations . . . it makes you want to learn more about your
topic. . . .

—Student

Asking Cityview School students to describe what they do online
was much like asking a diverse group of teenagers how they spend their
free time. The students use the Internet to take advantage of countless
convenient opportunities to play highly specialized online games, commiserate with other teens about sensitive adolescent concerns, gain
work experience, stay informed of current events, and grapple with the
social issues they will face in their adult lives. Although at times it may
appear that students are engaged only in entertainment, they consistently use constructivist learning strategies throughout these Internet-
mediated activities. As the boundaries between play and work blur in
their Internet use, Cityview teens find that learning is fun.

It is no surprise that the Internet holds entertainment appeal for
teens. Online, Cityview students gain quick, easy access to information about the latest cinema movies, popular music stars, and promi-
nent sports figures. Daryn, a basketball player, frequently visits the

official Web site of the National Basketball Association (NBA). "I just like the sports part of [the Internet]," he says. "I'm a big basketball fan, so I go to the NBA . . . to just see how people are doing." He is more interested in the individual players than in a particular team and likes this Web site because ". . . it shows you different posters, like different players." Unlike the newspaper, which often goes to press long before the latest scores are available, online sports reports feature up-to-the-minute results and action photographs from events worldwide.

Carla visits the same basketball site frequently during indoor recess time, but for different reasons. As the boys at the next computer gently tease Carla and her computer partner, Stacey, the girls debate which of two basketball stars—Kobe Bryant or Allen Iverson—is more attractive:

> CARLA [POINTING TO A PHOTOGRAPH OF BASKETBALL STAR KOBE BRYANT ON THE SCREEN]: What did you do, boy? I know you didn't look like that now. I'm going to get me a Kobe Bryant poster. See, there are so many more pictures [scrolls down the screen, then clicks so that a new screen appears]. Here are some more pictures. [Clicks on a picture, causing enlargement of that picture to appear on the screen. The other students who have gathered around the computer laugh.]
>
> CARLA: It [Bryant's photograph] is just looking bad on the computer.
>
> STACEY: Go back, go back.
>
> [Carla clicks on back button, causing computer screen to return to Los Angeles Lakers site.]
>
> STACEY [IN DISGUST]: Taking pictures like that! Tell me that don't look like a mug shot!
>
> CARLA [READS FROM SCREEN]: "Iverson world."
>
> STACEY: See, Iverson [Stacey's favorite NBA player at the moment] got his own world.
>
> CARLA: Kobe got his own universe.
>
> STACEY: Kobe got his own mug shot! [Laughs.]

Carla ignores Stacey's last comment and selects her favorite photograph from among the recently updated pictures of Kobe Bryant to print out for use as a poster.

Basketball players are not the only celebrities the girls follow online. Web sites featuring contemporary musicians and Hollywood movie stars are popular among Cityview students. Carla and Natalie are both infatuated with Leonardo DiCaprio, the lead actor in the season's best-selling cinema movie *Titanic*. Carla's obsession with the teen idol is beginning to wear off, but she acknowledges that she has spent a fair amount of time at *Titanic* Web sites. "Like *Titanic* is sort of boring me now," she says, "But . . . before I was obsessed with it . . ." When I ask what about these sites appeals to her, she admits with a sheepish grin that it is the male stars. ". . . [I]t's for the people," she says. ". . . Oh, I don't care about the boat . . . All I care about is one solitary person that is on that boat or on that team."

Unlike Carla, Natalie does not have Internet access at home. Still, she has become adept in her school computer use and is able to manage multitasking well enough to maneuver back and forth between Web sites related to her social studies project and *Titanic* sites. She smiles as she describes her favorite Internet use and admits to having used a movie star site on school time: "I like looking up like Leonardo DiCaprio. . . . You just look up . . . their name. . . . There was this one [Web site]—I was just looking at it right now." Although Natalie has seen the movie only twice, she sees her favorite movie star daily by visiting these Web sites. As she works on her social studies project on immigration into the United States during the 1930s, she keeps Leonardo DiCaprio always just one click of the mouse away.

Just as it is a source of information on movie stars, the Internet provides Cityview teens with the latest information on their favorite contemporary music performers. The Beck site is one of Jeff's favorite Web sites ". . . because he's my favorite performer and I find [out] about like you know what he's doing: where the next show's going to be, what are the next albums are going to be." Lori likes to search online for lyrics of favorite songs:

> I look for like mostly um stuff with music—I really like music.
> I just look for lyrics or pages. . . . I usually search for the pages

that have lyrics, cuz I like to sing, so I got the words to the song on the pages. . . . I'll look for a specific artist and then I'll see what song I like that they have.

Not all of these Web sites are "official" sites sponsored by the performers or their recording studios; in fact, Lori believes that many of the sites are created by other fans her age. For accuracy, she will compare these sites with her prior knowledge of the songs. Neither Jeff nor Lori attends all the concerts and purchases every album, but knowing the latest information on music stars is important to teens. The Internet is their source for that information.

Over the past two decades, American teens have become a major segment of the retail market. Product information is important to these teens as they choose how to utilize their purchasing power. Daryn points out that, in the case of a new name-brand razor, the Internet provides more comprehensive and timely information than does television:

> . . . [I]t took 'em 10 years to build it and they had, they're gonna have a big opening, but when you go on the Internet, you can see it before it comes out. They have the commercials on the Internet, so if you press a button it shows you the first commercial and it's pretty neat. . . . You can see—like [on] TV sometimes the products are far away, like on the screen, but when you're on the computer, if you want you can [look] close-up without going blind or without your ears hurting. . . . You can see more of the different details on the product. Like in the back, it just looks like one certain shaving stick or razor, but like when you're on the computer you can see the different things. . . .

Online, the students feel they are in control. By choosing which buttons on the Web site to click on, the Internet user decides how much or how little of the advertisement to view.

During the time I spent at Cityview, buying and selling via the Internet was still new. Online credit card transactions were popularly viewed as highly susceptible to fraud. At the time, Cityview students preferred local malls and mail-order catalogs to the Internet for shopping. They do, however, see this new mode of shopping as a possibility in their future. Although they are hesitant to spend their money on the Internet, they are more than willing to acquire items at no cost online. Students frequently mention "free stuff" as one of the attractions of the Internet. Lori and Kerri both use the Internet as a source of decorations for their bedrooms. Collecting decorations for her bedroom is not Lori's first choice of Internet use, but it is a good alternative to the more appealing chat rooms, which she is not allowed to use in school:

> I don't have a computer at home, so I use the one at school, so we can't use the chat room and stuff. . . . And that's like the basically only thing—or like I use it to like find cartoon characters and stuff on the Web. . . . [I]f they're cute, I'll print them out and I have this collage thing that I put it all on. . . .

Lori finds images of her favorite cartoon characters by going to the art section of a popular children's Web browser.

Kerri talks about the Internet as a space in which she can still play, even though she is supposed to be growing up:

> . . . I don't like to grow up. I'm not a person that grows up really fast. . . . I do grow mentally, but I don't grow mature. . . . I *can* be serious, but I *like* to be a kid, and so you find me going into [Web sites] like Looney Tunes. . . . I don't think you'll find a teenager going to Looney Tunes or cartoons. . . . But, see, I like to stay in touch with my little kid side.

Like Lori, Kerri has a "big collage" on her bedroom wall, which includes images of her favorite Looney Tunes cartoon character, Tweetie-Bird. But she likes the wide range of choices available to her online and includes other movie characters in her collage as well: "You can get pictures of Cinderella and stuff. I like stuff like that. That's really fun to look at cuz then you print them out and hang them up on your wall." Using images they obtain free from the Internet, these students create highly personalized collages to replace the stock posters that their parents purchased in mall novelty stores when the adults were teens.

Gabriel, still a beginner on the Internet, saves money by using the Web to ". . . look up codes for video games and stuff like that." He used to have a subscription to a video game magazine but ". . . ended it cuz it was expensive." In contrast to the video game magazines, which cost more than Gabriel can afford, the codes are free online. Mark uses his sophisticated technical skills to download program files from the Internet. ". . . I can download things," he says, "So like hacking programs, cuz I know some sites for that, and just like, download music. There's a, there's a site where you can download like music samples and so I . . . go to that site." I was familiar with the Web sites for popular musicians and recording studios that offer the music samples as a marketing strategy but asked Mark to tell me more about the "hacking programs." What he described was a typical teenagers' prank:

> Well for example there's these things where you could, um—it plays a sound and then you get to make a phone call from the— okay, um, it's like making free phone calls from the pay phone so when you drop in the quarter in the pay phone, it makes a special noise and then it gives you—it has the noises for the thing, so you could record the noise with a tape recorder and then try it. . . . I tried it, but it didn't work. [laughs]

In this use of the Internet, Mark was engaged in the 1990s version of pranks an earlier generation used to try to release large amounts of change from pay phones.

For Cityview students, the line between work and play is sometimes blurred online. The group of boys who designed Web sites as part of their eighth-grade mastery project assume that others will enjoy the Web sites that they find humorous and incorporate these sites into their final project. Jeff, who created a Web site on corporate greed in the United States, added links from his Web site to his favorite humorous sites, "the naked dancing llama" and "the really big button that doesn't do anything." He explained why he likes these sites:

> . . . [W]hat happened was, when you go there it has this weird little jingle music and it's got the naked llama . . . well, it's not really naked, but it's just a llama in a car and it's really funny, and I like little pointless Web pages like that and the really, really big button that doesn't do anything, cuz there's this *huge* button and you press this button and true to [its] name it does- n't do anything and so [the Web site] gives you all these stories

about these people . . . who are like really freaked out by the really big button that doesn't do anything . . . [in a deep mocking tone] "I press it and then it doesn't do anything and then, and then—" [returns to his earlier conversational tone] And it's like the best Web page I've ever seen. . . .

For these students, the Internet allows for a mix of humor and serious learning. Through their use of links on their Web sites, these students provide a source of entertainment as well as information for the prospective users of their sites.

Cityview students enjoy a wide variety of activities that depend primarily on the information functions of the Internet, but they are most excited about the possibilities presented when these information functions are combined with Internet communication tools. Early in my research, I was intrigued by Cityview students' constant use of the word *they* in their descriptions of different Web sites. Kristen, a beginning Internet user, does this as she describes a major online bookstore as a site that she considers easy to use:

. . . [Y]ou can look for a book like by title, um keyword, author—things like that. . . . And they have like, um, a *variety* of different books on every subject and you go on and you can find a book and then I think there's a possible way that you can like buy the book through the Internet and get it sent to you. . . .

To Kristen,

. . . a site that would be easy would have um directions that were easy to read . . . something with straightforward instructions and there's things that would say like "click here" and they would have like topics that you can click on which you understand.

Conversely, Jeff describes the type of Web site that is most likely to frustrate him as one that does not actually provide the information promised:

. . . [A] lot of pages are a waste of your time cuz they keep telling you they're going to bring you to all of this stuff, but they bring you to thousands of places and you never see any of it. It's like, okay, "We have like, we have all these fast facts about [a major entertainment corporation]" and you keep looking and looking and you just can't find it and there's just really badly made pages and it's frustrating.

In describing a wide variety of Web sites, Cityview students repeatedly referred to an indefinite "they," which was somehow connected with the Web site.

Initially, I applied an adult interpretation to this pattern and assumed that the students were assigning agency—the ability to act on its own, independent of human control—to the computer. As with other technological innovations, one of the phenomena that have accompanied the widespread use of the microcomputer is the assignment of human qualities and capabilities to the computer. Many a customer has phoned a billing agency to report an error, only to be told that "the computer did it." The implication is that a computer operating independently of any human control made the mistake. At Cityview, I assumed that the pronoun *they* referred to the computer itself and that these teens, like adults who had not grown up with computers, were assigning human capabilities to the various Web sites.

When Jeff decided to email the designer of a Web site that he found to be poorly maintained, I discovered that "they" were the designers of each site. For these students, each Web site is a direct link to and means of communication with its designer, another real person. Each Web site represents an opportunity for Cityview students to meet others who share their interests. Chat rooms and email, too, provide the students with daily opportunities for instant communication worldwide. Colin explains that this is why he has become a frequent Internet user, because "it's better than standing out on the street corner because . . . there are a lot of *good* people out there, and a lot of *great* kids. . . ." Like the shopping mall of the 1970s, the Internet has become a popular meeting place for today's teens. The difference is that the Internet allows students to be independent of parental transportation and still meet other teens worldwide.

When Cityview students go online with the purpose of meeting others, Internet searching tools enable the students to be efficient in their efforts to locate others who share their interests. Lynn, who has no sisters with whom to share the typical concerns of teenage girls, likes to go to sites intended specifically for girls. ". . . [T]here are a lot of home pages out there like, made especially for girls that you can look around," she says. Part of the appeal of these sites, Carla says, is that ". . . they're *not* made for boys." One of Lynn's favorites is the Web site for a popular girls' clothing brand. Although the site is intended to advertise the clothing, Lynn, along with Carla and Sarah, are all more interested in the ". . . whole bunch of stories and stuff" that can also be found on this site. Sarah describes the site as being "like a magazine" but, as Lynn points out, with the added value of being able to ask peers for advice on concerns such as "the sensitive boy thing."

Chat rooms are a popular online meeting space for these Cityview girls. Sarah tends to make new acquaintances each time she goes online:

> Sometimes I meet up with the same people, but it's kind of hard to meet up with the same people unless you go to like the same exact chat room—it would be like "Come back here next week," or something.

Sarah does not have a single favorite chat room. Instead, she moves about between different online spaces in much the same way that teens hoping to meet others at the mall drift from one spot to another. "I usually go—I don't have a good one [chat room] that I go to . . . I just kind of like mix around and find a good place and just stay there . . ."

Carla uses instant messaging to make friends on the Internet. As described in chapter four, *Instant messaging* is a term used to describe synchronous email, which is similar to a telephone conversation in that both parties in the conversation are online simultaneously. She has even arranged boy-girl dates online. "I instant message them," she describes, "Cuz like you can have dates over the Inter[net]—you know, like '7:00 on Saturday; make sure you're on,' and stuff." Unlike a high school mixer, there is no public embarrassment for Carla if she does not meet any boys in a particular online session. Likewise, if she is approached by a boy she does not like, there is no awkward disentanglement from the conversation. She simply ceases to email him.

Meetings in chat rooms and via instant messaging are not always left to chance. Colin describes how he lists his profile online to enhance his chances of meeting others with whom he is compatible. Listing his interest in RPGs in his personal profile provides Colin with the opportunity to meet other teens who share this pastime:

> [The Internet's] also a great recreational tool. It gives you more opportunities to meet people. Especially to meet people— because I get IM's [instant messages] often, just, um, someone who's read my profile, like, for example, someone looked up, put in the key word Riverview in the profiles and brought up mine and he IM'd me, "Hey, I was from Riverview, too, and I liked RPG's . . ."

In this way, Colin meets friends with whom he can play the RPGs, either online or in more conventional face-to-face meetings. The purposefulness of Colin's personal profile does not prevent him from receiving extraneous messages: ". . . so sometimes they [other Internet users] put in something—[laughs] like I get IM'd by girls a lot. They say, you know, 'Hey, 14F here,'—you know— 'wanta chat?'"

Colin maintains that the Internet is a very efficient way to meet others. To support his claim, he describes a recent online encounter:

> Like, I met this one girl—I didn't even really meet her. She was in the same room talking to a friend of mine and I was over there for my friend and I like saw her briefly and I didn't even really remember her and then a couple of months later, she IM'd me. She said, you know, "Are you Colin?" and I was like, "Yeah," and she said, "Ralph [a mutual friend] told me you were online." . . . I didn't even remember what she looked like, but I got to know her, you know, online.

Although Colin had been physically situated in the same room with this girl at his friend's party, he did not meet her, yet online, where there are millions of Internet users present at any given time, she found him.

The Internet is more than an electronic playground where students meet with their peers to play games and gossip. It is also their workspace. Online, Cityview students use Internet communication and information functions for a variety of serious purposes. These range from providing each other with online technical assistance to following updates on current social issues. Mark, for example, has not yet reached high school but is already working online as an amateur technical support specialist. One service he provides to friends is checking game files transferred across the Internet for viruses:

> Actually, I have this friend—he doesn't really have a virus detector so he sends them to me [via email] and asks me if they have viruses. And so I check them, but he gives 'em to me also, so it's not like he just asks me. If I ask for some programs, he gives them to me and says, "Tell me if it has a virus or not." . . .

At times, this work becomes frustrating:

> . . . it's just that um lots—people come up to me and go "How do you do this?" and "How do you do that?" And not really like in school people, but other friends that email me, and I say, "Just look around and see what it does, cuz that's how I did it," and then I keep getting email back and it gets me kind of—like, they keep on asking me and it's right there if you look around. . . .

He explained further the source of his frustration:

> Well, I—even if I tell them, they, they still probably do the wrong thing. . . . When somebody emails me and asks me how to do this on the computer, like to move a file or something, and I tell them and it still doesn't work and they ask me the same question again and I'll probably tell them for the second time and then after that I just don't listen to them.

On the Internet, it doesn't matter that Mark is only a teenager with no formal credentials as a computer technician. Nor does he need to rely on his parents for transportation to and from each service stop he makes. All that counts online is his proven expertise. As he helps his friends to activate and maintain their computer games, Mark is developing valuable work experience for the types of jobs available to students growing up in an information economy.

Cityview students use the Internet to follow current social and political topics that concern them. Ariella's favorite Web sites are "anything . . . having to do with the real life images that are going on in the world." Jeff prefers his Internet service provider's news service over television news:

> . . . [L]ike when I hear something on the news or something and I'm curious about it, I'll go find out about that. Cuz it's always updated there, so it's not like you have to wait like hours until the next show comes on. . . . Usually you just go to news and it has all the big things going on and you just click on whatever one you want.

The convenience and user control inherent in Internet technology make it an appealing news source for students. Television as a broadcast medium requires the user to wait for information on any given topic. As an interactive technology, the Internet enables students to select for immediate delivery only the news on topics of interest to them. Instead of watching a half-hour evening news broadcast, students can spend a few minutes each day at their convenience to get updates on the local and world events they choose to follow.

What students learn online may have consequences in their offline activities. Jeff relied heavily on the Internet for information for his mastery project on contemporary corporate greed. One problem he identified as he browsed Web sites about a major discount department store was the underrepresentation of minorities: ". . . I went to the actual [store Web site] and I counted the number of minorities in their catalog and there was like 2, compared to like 25, 30 people. . . ." He followed up his survey of the store's online catalog by using the company's Web site to request that a print catalog be mailed to his home. He then conducted the same survey using the print catalog to test the conclusion he had arrived at using the online catalog.

Jeff later encountered a personal dilemma as a result of this project. When his parents finally agreed to buy him a backyard trampoline he had wanted for months, he discovered that this piece of sports equipment was least expensive at this same discount department store. In his research paper, Jeff stated,

> As it is corporations are dependent on us. If we don't buy anything from them they go out of business. But if a corporation

grows too large, we will become dependent on that corporation; they'll have control over us. We need some certain products to survive, and if a store has a monopoly on a product, we will need to go to that store. We will be forced to support that corporation, whether we like it or not.

From his online research, he had learned about boycotting as a means of preventing the continued growth of large corporations. He was faced with the choice of either following his own recommendation that consumers "don't buy whatever you need at [the discount department store], buy it at a small store instead" or supporting the large retail company he eschewed. On the Internet, he had learned that "everything in the world is dependent on people" and that his decision had an impact, however small, on the power base of large corporations. For Jeff and his classmates, the Internet is more than an electronic game room. On the Internet, students at 12 and 13 years old have countless convenient opportunities to gain work experience, stay informed on current events, and grapple with the social issues they will face in their adult lives.

As exciting as the Internet may be, for Cityview students it does not substitute for offline experience and social interaction. Instead, the technology expands both the range of activities and the pool of potential work and play partners conveniently available to students. None of the Cityview students spends excessive amounts of time online. School, homework, and other extracurricular activities limit their weekday use. Jeff, one of the most fluent Internet users at Cityview, estimates that he uses the Internet for about three hours per week, mostly as a rainy day activity. When I asked him what he would do if he were not online during that time, he responded, "Probably sit around. Maybe watch TV or something, cuz I usually only go on the Internet when it's rainy and I can't be outside." For teens growing up with computers, the Internet simply expands the range of activities possible on any given day.

Online, learning and fun are not mutually exclusive. Throughout these Internet-mediated activities, Cityview students consistently use constructivist learning strategies. Online, students collaborate with others to solve authentic problems they have identified. Colin, for example, first learned about Web page design from an online friend who shares his interest in a particular RPG. Instead of taking a class or reading a manual on Web sites, Colin is learning how to construct a site through collaboration with another teen hundreds of miles away. Although their site's focus on Mario RPGs does not fit with what educators typically consider important topics for middle school students to learn, Colin is developing sophisticated online skills, which he then applies to his schoolwork.

Mark is usually quiet and reserved offline and tends to be a loner in the classroom. But on the Internet, he initiates collaboration with others who share his interests in the technical features of computers:

> Cuz [my Internet service provider] has this thing called "instant message," so you just type in—you respond right back—it's not like email. It's just like talking. . . . I have some other friends and I talk to them, cuz they also are into computer stuff.

He first learned about the hacking sites he likes from an online friend: ". . . [F]irst my friend he told me like 'I'm learning how to hack and everything,' and then I just typed in 'hacking' and it gave me all these lists of everything." Online, Mark is able to identify quickly and easily others who share his specialized interests. The Internet is not a substitute for offline friendships; offline, Mark most likely would have remained a loner with or without the Internet.

Online learning is embedded in social interaction. The minute Cityview students log on to the Internet, they are connected to others far beyond their classroom or homes. At times, this creates an urgency for students to learn new skills that does not exist in a conventional classroom setting. Prior to using the Internet, Colin had made several attempts to learn proper keyboarding skills. In addition to formal classroom lessons, he had tried a self-tutorial computer software program. He was frustrated by the computer program: ". . . [I]t said like, I typed 20 words per minute and I'm like 'No! I type much faster than that!' But it said, 'But do you type *correctly*?' What does it matter if I type correctly?" Once Colin began to use the Internet, his desire to participate in chat rooms and instant messaging drove a sudden increase in his typing speed:

> . . . [J]ust talking, um, chatting makes it necessary for you to be able to type fast, to get your ideas across fast. Because I was in an IM with a girl the other day and I was reading my

mail at the same time and she said you know, "You don't seem like you want to chat." And I said, "Why so?" And she said, "Because you are taking so long to respond." . . . [Y]ou really need to be able to get your ideas across quickly. . . .

Colin might never have learned to type with only a school grade or feedback from a computer tutorial as his only motivation. But when his ability to interact with online peers was at stake, mastering the typing skills became critical to him.

At the same time that the Internet provides students with a means to collaborate with those who share their interests, it also exposes students to a wide variety of perspectives on any given topic. Earlier in the school year, three of the eighth-grade boys had created a HyperCard presentation on the architectural history in the neighborhood immediately surrounding Cityview School. Mark described how his group used a variety of real estate Web sites to include additional examples of architectural elements in the project:

> . . . [I]t's where they sell houses and they gave . . . an example of each of the houses that we were looking for . . . that's where we got most of the houses from and others for example, some features of the houses, we just found some regular pictures that people they just took of their own houses. . . .

When I asked Mark how his group decided which of the many real estate Web sites to look at, he replied, "I went through all of 'em and I just look at the pictures that we needed and then we chose maybe which pictures were the best to use. . . ."

In researching the assassination of United States President John F. Kennedy for his project, Rickie found so many Web sites on this topic that he struggled to decide what to use and when to conclude the project. After being exposed to a multitude of theories on the assassination, Rickie took the sophisticated point of view that, since the assassination, Kennedy had taken on mythical proportions in American politics. In the research paper that accompanied his Web site on Kennedy, Rickie used several of Kennedy's policies and decisions to support the conclusion that he was not an unqualified "defender of liberal ideas." Through their use of the Internet, these students discover their world to be far more complex than that presented in their middle school social studies textbook.

During the final quarter of the year, each Cityview student used the Internet to research a topic of the student's choice and then completed an interdisciplinary "mastery project" on this topic. Six students designed Web pages as one component of the final project. For these six students, the Internet provides a dynamic medium through which to represent their ideas. The group agrees with Jeff's explanation of why creating a Web site is more fun than a conventional paper or offline project:

> . . . [T]here's more, more technical stuff you have to do instead of just writing it on the page of paper and laying it out. . . . Instead of everything being manual, it's sort of magical, like, instead of you turning the page—there's no surprise basically when you turn the page—but when you click on something you didn't think would be there and it brings you to something and it has everything laid out there, I just, I don't know, I like that.

Rickie adds that the Web site gives him "more freedom" to demonstrate his understanding of his research topic. "So, like in art," he explains, "you have a certain limit to go to, like you can't draw this [or] this, but like in a computer, you can do just about anything, so you could do a lot." Justin adds that, unlike a research paper, their online projects show "more personality." The boys agree that, through the use of a variety of multimedia tools and links to other sites, they can convey as much or as little of their personalities as they choose. In designing these Web sites, the students come to see their learning as a highly personalized endeavor that is closely intertwined with their sense of self.

Online learning is not without risks for these students. Cityview students are well aware that any project in the form of a Web site may reach a far wider audience than a single teacher. The students are constantly thinking of this audience as they work on their projects. Jeff includes in his Web site on corporate greed features that he feels will appeal to a variety of users:

> My page just goes all over the place, like most people's home pages. . . . Basically, I'm just gonna tell my friends and family

to look at it just for fun, and then anybody else who stumbles across it can have a good time.

He was slightly hesitant, however, about including in the section about himself a link to his favorite comic book because ". . . it's like this underground comic book. . . . And it's a really, really funny comic book, but it's way too violent for most people. . . ." Colin was sure to include links to sites where interested Web users could purchase the books that he had used in his project on astrology. Rickie was sensitive to his audience's tolerance for violence and chose not to include a link to a site on the Kennedy assassination that featured a riflery target superimposed on a human silhouette. "Ohhh—that's a bit much!" he said, as he moved on to another Web site.

When the students selected the formats for their final projects, none of the girls chose to create Web sites. When I asked Carla, Sarah, and Lynn about this, their initial explanation was that they just weren't interested. But then Sarah speculated on another possible reason that none of the girls is involved in the Web page project: ". . . I think the girls just pick topics that it wouldn't fit. . . ." The girls explained further that their lack of participation in this project had more to do with a sense that their research topics would hold little interest for a wider online audience:

SARAH: . . . [L]ike when you make a Web page you want it to be interesting, not boring. Some of our topics would have been really boring. Like yours [looks at Carla and laughs]—like "The Big Bang Theory" [in slow, dull mocking voice].

CARLA [PROTESTS]: Mine would have been interesting if I had [made a Web page]. I could've added a lot of stuff.

SARAH: Like you really need a lot of pictures.

LYNN: Yeah, you need a lot of pictures for the Web page. . . . Linda [a classmate who was doing a project on weather] could've done the Web page, but all she could've had on there was like a whole bunch of pictures of clouds and you need more than just clouds. You need different pictures.

Sarah maintains that, for a successful Web site project, the students need to be thinking about the audience even before they decide on their research topics. You need to have a topic, she says,

> . . . that would make people want to read it, because like . . . some things [Web sites] you like click on the thing, and say, "This looks like sooo boring." It's just like words, writing all the way down the page. There's no pictures or anything, so you're like "Oh, I don't want to waste my time reading this." . . . Like if you're . . . sitting there on the Net and you see this title and it's just like, "The Weather" . . . you're like, "That doesn't look interesting." . . . You already know the weather is the weather—it just sits there [laughs].

Although these students never indicated any concern about who would read their conventional research papers, they were very much aware of the potential audience for their Web pages. Throughout the design process, they were constantly responding to what they anticipated to be the expectations of an online audience that was very real to them.

The most difficult aspect of the Web page project was bringing it to a close at the end of the school year. The combination of Internet and microcomputer technology makes it easy for students to continue researching their topics and adding to their Web sites indefinitely. According to Jeff, "That's what's cool" about Web page design. On another occasion, he explained that one of the things he liked best about working on this project was that the computer and Internet make learning convenient. With as little as 30 seconds, he said, ". . . you can just hop over to the computer and . . . just you know, do one thing, type something up whenever you want. . . ." Each Web site contains links that lead students to additional Web sites on the topic. Using this process, Ricky became engrossed in his project on President John F. Kennedy's assassination. Ricky explained what he liked best about designing his own Web page:

> . . . I think the Web pages are good because . . . because um you get to—when you start designing it and doing all those kinds of crazy decorations . . . it makes you want to learn more about

your topic, it makes you want to go out and get more information and get more pictures. . . .

Right up until the final exhibition night, students continued revising their Web sites in between graduation festivities. The "really cool" part of learning online is that it is an open-ended process of constant revision of one's understanding. Learning is limited only by the student's interest in the topic pursued and is not dependent on the availability of resources in the student's immediate physical surroundings.

6

INFORMATION
AND MISINFORMATION

STUDENTS' ONLINE RESEARCH

I would probably have to look into three other [Web sites] just
in case the information isn't correct and um, but . . . if I knew
something about the topic . . . I can go, "oh, wait this is true,"
"this is true," "this is true," and "I've seen this before." . . .
                                                              —Student

As the rapid development of Internet technology has made the creation and maintenance of Web sites increasingly simple and inexpensive,
the volume of information available online has increased exponentially.
Teachers in "wired" classrooms face new challenges. Although Web sites
are highly attractive to students, the Internet is not the most appropriate
information resource for every research project. Students may find, for
instance, that it is far easier to locate a broad overview of a particular historical period in an encyclopedia than on the Internet. The teacher's first
challenge is to help students determine whether the Internet or other
materials, such as books, newspapers, and magazines, best fit the
research question at hand. If students opt to use the Internet, they may
need guidance in locating the information they really need from the vast
number of Web sites now online. In addition, teachers fear that students
will select Web sites designed by individuals with little or no credentialed
expertise on the topic. A Web site featuring the periodic table minus one

element, for example, has become part of educators' lore surrounding the new technology. With the massive volume of information available on the Internet comes the worry that students will not distinguish between information and misinformation.

Teachers at Cityview School incorporate student Internet use into school research projects but maintain reservations about the information their students gather from the World Wide Web. One teacher expressed concern that student Web searching consumes large amounts of classroom time:

> It can take a whole period before [the students] really find something that is valuable to them, and it is frustrating when they don't have enough time because it's like, "Okay, I just spent this whole time and I just got started and I haven't gotten anywhere. I haven't found anything that's really useful."

Cityview places a strong emphasis on student research skills at all grade levels. During the first half of the eighth grade, teachers focus on the skills that students will need to complete the eighth-grade mastery project, a major interdisciplinary research project that serves as one of Cityview's prerequisites for promotion to high school. Still, the teachers worry about their students' ability to sift through the information on the Web:

> There's a real issue of discerning what is a good site and what is too technical for them or what is not really quite on the topic or . . . "What's a neat site where I can get a lot of ideas and information from?"

One of this teacher's fears is what happened with one assignment earlier in the year. According to the teacher, certain Web sites became "trendy" among students. "Once kids found out that there were good sites," the teacher observed, "that's what they searched stuff with, and there wasn't much going out and looking for other sites."

As pointed out by a Cityview teacher who attended college during the 1980s, most educators completed their own formal schooling prior to the widespread dissemination of the Internet. With the introduction of the Internet into the classroom, teachers face the challenge of guiding students through a far greater volume of information than that which was previously available to the teachers themselves. In contrast to the print resources the teachers used in their own grade school studies, today's teenagers have convenient access to information in a variety of exciting multimedia formats. In order to help students develop effective information skills, teachers need to know what strategies students use to find their way through the information explosion of the late 20th century. In 1998, I had the opportunity to observe Cityview students navigate the Internet and to learn from them what criteria they use to select the information that they feel is most valid for their personal and school-related information needs.

For Cityview students, convenience is a key factor in their decision to use the Internet over other conventional classroom resources. Despite their teachers' concerns about the difficulty of sifting through all the information available online, students maintain that the Web is far more convenient than the library. Natalie, who is a relative newcomer to the Internet, describes the Internet and library as being very similar when it comes to school research projects. "I think you can find the same thing you can find in the library on the Internet," she explains, "because I think they both have the same information on like basically any topic." The Internet, however, is more convenient:

> [The Internet's] different because it's close by and . . . it's like easier to find stuff on there because like if you are in the library you have to get up and walk through a place and find the computer and all that stuff, and on the Internet you . . . surf through the sites that come up and you find what you need. . . .

Gabriel, also relatively inexperienced with the Internet, obtained some books and magazine articles from the library for his mastery project, but he finds the Web more convenient. Using the Internet, he said, "was a lot easier . . . because we just got to click on the stuff and not have to go walk around the entire library just to find a couple of books. . . ." Gabriel went on to explain that he is often disappointed when he is unable to locate on the shelf books listed in the library catalog. Recently, he returned frustrated from the public library after finding only one book on his topic. "Some of the other books [in the catalog] looked really good," he said, "but they weren't there for some reason."

Jeff is very pragmatic in his reasons for choosing the Internet over the library for school research projects. Jeff has a home computer with Internet access and is a far more experienced Internet user than either Natalie or Gabriel. Getting to the library is very simple for Jeff: "[T]here's a library near my house now so it makes it convenient." But he still prefers the Internet because "you don't get overdue fines on the Internet. . . . I just had to go pay off 12 bucks on my [library] card, and so, [the Internet's] a lot nicer." Jeff's parents require him to pay his own overdue fines at the library but do not require him to contribute to the monthly fee for home Internet service. As is to be expected of any active teenagers, Cityview students do not want to spend all their time on school research projects. In choosing the information resources they use for these assignments, students place a very high priority on convenience and ease of use.

The students do not depend solely on the Internet for their project information. As part of the eighth-grade mastery project, each student completes a five-page research paper on a topic of the student's choice. The students' bibliographies include a wide variety of books, newspaper and magazine articles, videotapes and personal interviews, in addition to Web sites. Students recognize that, depending on the particular information needed, the Internet may not always be the best resource. At one point, three girls were working on a social studies project on the American Revolutionary War. When Kristen called out to her partners that she was unable to find anything about the Battles of Lexington and Concord on the Internet, one partner, Lynn, pointed out to her, "The Internet won't work for this type of thing. What we need is an encyclopedia because it gives us the main points."

Although Cityview students rely heavily on the Internet for resources related to school projects and personal interests, they are skeptical of information on the Web. They recognize that anyone can publish online. They know that electronic publication lacks the expense and editing process that help to prevent false information from being published in traditional print formats:

> JEFF: . . . Well, cuz it costs money to publish and make books, so you want to know what you're talking about. . . . I'm not gonna say, "Oh, well, I'm gonna write a false book today about how carrots are—" I don't know—
>
> JUSTIN: —green.
>
> JEFF: Yeah, carrots are green. And you just put "carrots are green." And you could publish a thousand books, but it would cost you so much money and no one would buy it. . . . Web pages are a lot more inexpensive and easier to produce and . . . easier to, to fool people. Because with books, you know, you put your face, where you got your sources, what you're doing. They can look in the back before they buy it. But in a Web page, you know—it's just, "here's the stuff, believe it if you want." . . .
> They don't have the author of this Web site or they don't have to make a thousand copies of it.

Cityview students know that no special credentials are required for a person to publish online. They assume that, when they are searching the Web, it is their own responsibility to weed out potentially unreliable information.

Students are particularly suspicious of information conveyed in personal Web sites—that is, sites mounted by individuals with no corporate or organizational backing. Kerri is typical of Cityview students in her distrust of personal Web pages. When I asked her how she selects which sites to look at if her Web search generates a long list of sites, she explained that she starts by avoiding all the personal Web pages: ". . . I wouldn't go to a site that's like 'my page.' Sometimes it's like someone's page of something—like 'Joanna's page for the Titanic'—I don't really go for that. . . ." She makes a distinction between her feelings toward the person who authored the site and her concerns about the quality of the information:

> Like, it doesn't really matter to me, like . . . how old is this person . . . or is this a boy or a girl or is this person, you know from—where is this person [from]. . . . I really don't care about that. . . . [W]hat goes in my mind is, is this person telling the truth? Is this person [giving] real facts? Or did this person just make all these facts?

She explained that she uses a personal Web page only if she is willing to spend the time to compare the information on that site with other sources or if she has some prior knowledge of the topic:

> I would probably have to look into three other ones just in case the information isn't correct and um, but . . . if I knew *anything* about a topic, I wouldn't go to a home page that says "my," but if I knew something about the topic and I knew I can go, "oh wait this is true," "this is true," "this is true," and "I've seen this before," and "that I wasn't sure," too, but it looks like the home page is pretty good, I would then research back into it. But if it's like, "the Titanic was three feet" . . . or something like that, like I knew how big the Titanic was and I knew that wasn't correct, so that would mean it could be either a mistake and I would not trust the home page. Other mistakes that I would use in my report . . . would be *wrong*. . . . But I normally go for home pages that are maybe done by a company or something like that.

The students are not yet sophisticated enough in their information skills to recognize the potential biases in "official" or "company" Web sites. Jeff explained that he does not like to go to personal Web sites because ". . . that's not information, it's opinions." He recognizes this in part because of the Web site he himself has designed:

> . . . I don't like to go to people's personal sites cuz like my Web site's an opinion, so if they want info other than . . . facts about

[large corporations], then they shouldn't, you know, really come [to Jeff's Web site].

When I asked Jeff how he distinguishes "official" sites from personal Web pages, he explained, ". . . [O]n the [site] they can say, 'This is an official page.' Unless they say that, it's not [the official site]. There can only be one official page." He had a vague sense that there are legal ramifications that prevent Web site designers from falsely claiming to be the "official page":

> Cuz if you said, "This is the official Lakers page" . . . . first off you'd get sued by the Lakers, then by the online service, and then . . . by the company that made the Web page, so it would cause you a lot of trouble.

He went on to say that the Web search engine he uses most frequently sorts out the amateur personal Web pages:

> And anyway, people probably wouldn't believe you, cuz it would go under the home web page thing unless you were at a business. When you put a home Web page on the Net, it goes under the home Web page category. . . . There usually, cuz on Yahoo—it's a search engine . . . there's like "home Web pages." It's under like . . . homemade Web pages and then there's professional Web pages, you know, like Microsoft Web page or big things like that.

What neither Kerri nor Jeff appears to understand is that even the information found on Web sites that carry the authority associated with being an "official" or "company" site may not be totally reliable. Jeff, for example, does not appear to make any connection between the professional basketball team's use of an "official" Web site as a marketing tool and the way in which the team and individual players are presented on that site.

Cityview students associate the information on personal sites with the author or designer of the site. The students are quick to distinguish between fact and opinion in these Web sites. They are especially alert to the potential for personal opinions to be mixed with facts on Web pages in part because of their own experience designing Web pages. While Justin was working on his Web page on army tanks, he discussed with Andy and Colin whether he should include his opinion on each tank or limit the text to "just facts." In a later interview, the boys discussed how they arrived at the appropriate mix of fact and opinion for their respective research topics:

> JUSTIN: Um, mine, it doesn't have any opinion at all, so I had to get all the *facts,* like about the tanks, cuz I'm doing tanks, and . . . I had to get all the facts from books and stuff like that, so, like— pretty much except and a few times I put my opinions on tanks and that was me, but other than that I just got it from other places.
>
> JEFF: My page is strictly opinionated. I mean, I'm talking about how I hate corporations and how they all need to go away and stuff and I put—I back up my opinions with facts, like, you know, how [a large discount department store] like puts so many businesses out of business . . . but like the basis of my page it says on the top, "Welcome to my page; Corporations are pure evil." So it's like, I don't know, just more fun.

Justin went on to explain why he is reluctant to inject his opinion into the information he provides on his Web site:

> . . . I just figured that—I don't know, when I go to like a tank page or something that has opinions on stuff, I really don't trust it that much, because I mean, this like—this guy could be makin' it up and it could be just like what *he* thinks. He could be some weirdo and like with mine, I just wanted to put facts because facts can't be like *wrong*—well, they can, but you know what I mean. . . . I just didn't want people doubting my [descriptions].

As a result of their own experience designing Web pages, these students approach online information with caution. They are quick to recognize that there is nothing to prevent anyone—themselves included—from providing either biased or erroneous information on the Internet. The students associate the information with the author or designer of the site and are quick to distinguish between fact and opinion in Web sites. For these students, each Web site represents only one perspective on the topic discussed and is connected directly back to the person(s) posting the information. Cityview students test this information in the same way they might challenge one another in face-to-face discussions.

One strategy students use to evaluate online information is to compare it with other resources. When asked about the balance between facts and opinions in their own Web sites, students shifted the discussion topic to the validity of facts found on Web pages:

JEFF: But probably you could make up all those things—

JUSTIN: Yeah, but that's the problem—

JEFF: Yeah, I know you're not, but that's for all they know. That's why you're not going to other people's pages, because all—they could be thinking the same way as you "I'm only making facts for people," but—

INTERVIEWER: Yeah, and how do you know, like if you go to—if you get your facts from somebody else's Web site—how do you know that I didn't just sit down this afternoon and decide to make a Web site about tanks even though I know nothing about it?

ANDY: You don't know.

JUSTIN: Well, I got all the facts from books, but I got all the pictures from other Web sites.

Ricky and Colin also used Justin's strategy of relying on books for facts and Web sites for pictures. Books as the conventional offline information source have a static nature for Cityview students. In the students' views, the facts in books stand alone, apart from the author. Online, information is directly associated with the person who has made it available through a Web site. These students are reluctant to accept as fact online information they cannot substantiate using books.

Students do not make the same connection between the author and book that they make between the Web site designer and the information presented in the site. Kerri, for example, trusts that any book that contains inaccurate information is appropriately labeled:

> Cuz you have to watch out on the Internet, cuz anything can be given out on the Internet. As for books, that's another story. You can write almost anything you want, but then . . . it would be fiction. . . . [I]f it was non-true I don't think people would put it as a nonfiction book; I think they would put it as a fiction book. So then that's easy for me to say, "this is true" and "this is not." But on the Internet, they can put anything they want, so you have to watch out when you go on the Internet.

In their online lives, students see each Web site as the representation of one person or group's understanding. In contrast to library books that contain facts, each Web site is the product of the person(s) who designed the site. The author or designer of the site is a real person who is only an email message away from the students. Students take a discriminating approach to online information—in essence, challenging the person associated with the information by comparing it with the information in other sources and their own prior knowledge of the topic.

Students are also skeptical of visual information on the Web. Just as they do with online text, students use their prior knowledge to assess visual images they find on the Internet. When Daryn's Web search for information on an American Revolutionary War hero yielded several sites with pictures, Daryn checked with other members of his group before downloading the pictures to his project file. Pointing to the images on his screen, he asked his partners, "Do you know if Lafayette looks like any of these guys?" A group of girls working on the same social studies assignment discussed among themselves whether or not a particular image of Johnny Tremain was acceptable for use in their project. Just as Kristen quickly clicked past a screen showing information on Johnny Tremain, Lynn glanced over and protested, "But it's a good picture. Go back and print it out." Kristen returned to the previous screen and pointed out that the image is actually the cover photo on a Disney videotape. She asked Lynn, "Isn't that the picture of the actor and not the real person?" Lynn agreed, and the girls abandoned this image in an effort to find a more historically accurate portrayal. In these projects, the students recognized that the need for accurate information extends beyond text to include visual representation of their ideas.

This is not to say that all Cityview students habitually evaluate the information they find on the Internet. Although Gabriel had first used the Internet as part of a school Web site project a year earlier, he rarely used a computer in class and was not as fluent in his online searching as were some of his classmates. Gabriel was quick to accept as "good information" the data contained in a Web site on legalized gambling. When I asked him to clarify what he meant by "good information" on his research topic, he responded:

> . . . I mean for this project, I needed a lot of, like, statistics, mostly. That's what my paper is, so some of [the Web sites he used] just had paragraphs and just stuff that I didn't need and the other one had a bunch of statistics and it was a pretty big Web page. It had a bunch of different things that I could go to and find out all different things.

I probed further and asked how he knew if the statistics were accurate. "Well, I just trust and hope that they're good," he replied. This range of sophistication in Cityview students' assessment of online resources indicates a need for students to be challenged continually about how they select information for inclusion in their projects.

Anyone who has ever searched for information on the Web knows that the list of Web sites generated by a single search query may include hundreds or even thousands of sites. One of the questions that I explored with Cityview students was how they manage to find what they really need amid the massive volume of information available online. Jeff contends that it is not really difficult, once an Internet user has learned a few basic searching skills:

> You need to know where to go to search for stuff and then what to type in and then the tricks to get you to find the stuff, you

know, like the quotation marks and the plus sign[1] and all that stuff. And if you know what you're doing, basically, that's all you really need, is the search engine and all you have to do is read and double click and go wherever you want. . . . [I]t's sort of a simple concept. Once you can do sort of a certain amount of things, you can do pretty much anything with it.

Jeff says that his Cityview teachers introduced him to these skills, and then ". . . basically I learned everything else from my friends. And then we got a computer, so Mom could do typing. . . . Then I just sort of learned from there." Mark's experience is similar to Jeff's. "Actually, I think I started using it here first," he says, "and then we got the Internet service [at home]. So, but then I used it more at home cuz I wanted to."

The first step in a Web search is to decide which search engine to use. Internet users can choose from a wide variety of search engines, each of which enables the Internet user to search for information by keywords, date of publication, language, and a variety of other characteristics of online documents. The classroom computers at Cityview School are set to default to one particular commercial search engine. During their school Internet use, most students rely almost exclusively on this search engine. One of the teachers had taught students to use another search engine, which is designed specifically for children. This children's search engine provides a directory to "safe" Web-based resources closely related to topics typically studied in elementary and secondary school. I never observed students using the teacher-recommended children's search engine in school. Lori was the only student who mentioned using any children's search engine at all. She uses it at the local public library specifically to locate images of her favorite children's cartoon characters.

Occasionally, students use more than one search engine to gather information on a single topic. Mark explained that the search engine most Cityview students use features links to additional search engines. From the first search engine, he says, ". . . it takes me to Altavista, when there's like . . . more research, so I use that too." With the exception of Mark, Cityview students do not appear to be aware of the differences between the search engines readily available to them.

The students rely on the search engine to organize the results of each search in a way that helps them to select which Web sites to examine. Kerri explains that she uses the broader categories for searching provided by the search engine.

> I usually get like 60 [Web sites] . . . on Yahoo, they all, like if you go *all* the way to the bottom, they'll have another line that says like "search" and they'll have it like—how do you explain this? On the top of the page it's going to say, "search women's rights" . . . and then if you go to the bottom, you put in voting, so the top of the next page, you put "search women's rights," *boing!* Or you just put in the whole thing, or whatever.

She offers her understanding of how the search engine organizes the results of each search in a way that helps the Internet user to sift through the information available:

> It's usually . . . what they do is they give you one good site, like in highlight . . . like the first one is what they came up with . . . and then they have a list on the bottom and they say, "Here's the others," and then they have a list, something like that.

There are other factors involved in how Kerri decides which Web sites to look at first when her search yields a long list of possibilities:

> Sometimes, I just like press the button, just press and go down and something that catches my eye or new or something like the movement or history, I just click into it. Like it matters what I'm really going in for.

Jeff pointed out that, although the list of Web sites generated by a single search may be long, not all of the sites are relevant to the Internet user's research interest. Typically, the search engine will place sites that appear to be most relevant at the top of the list, which helps him to decide which sites to go to first:

> Well, [the search engine] organizes it. Like at the top, it's the one [Web site] with the most stuff about that, then farther

> down—But, you know, it says a hundred but probably the last
> 50 are about applesauce, you never know. . . .

But he cautioned that the organization of the list is not always reliable. He understands that this sorting is based primarily on words in the site titles, which at times may be misleading. ". . . [T]here's really no way to do it, though," he cautioned. "I mean it's really hard. They don't get to look through every page and see what it's about." The students depend on the organizational features of the search engine but realize that the computer user must still exercise some critical thinking to sort through the results of a Web search and determine which sites might prove most useful.

Cityview students use keywords in the title of each site as one method of determining whether or not the site might be a useful source of information. Colin looks to the name of the site for clues as to whether or not it is a source he might want to use. He explained how he sifted through the results of his Web search on astrology:

> . . . I put in astrology and I got a bunch of sites and there were
> a couple of them that were like that [irrelevant], you know, the
> psychic hotlines. But I just looked in the ones that were useful,
> that looked good. Like there was "astrology dash numerology
> dot com" and I went to that and that was very useful because
> that was about the different signs and stuff. There's a place—
> "Astrology World"—and I went there. . . . [Y]ou can usually
> tell from the name of the site, what kind of site it is.

I asked Colin for examples of how the titles help him to determine whether or not a site might be useful in his research. He explained that a site which uses *world* to describe itself, for instance, usually has an abundance of information:

> Well, if it says something else about astrology, like numerology,
> you can tell, and something like "Astrology World," it could
> have been the world of fortune telling is opened up to you, but
> to call itself a "world" it would have to be something else.

He knows that this method is not foolproof. As he points out, a site called "Astrology World" could be either an informational site or a commercial site selling online fortune-telling services.

Cityview students expect each Web site to include the information promised or implied by the title. They judge the integrity of the site in part on how closely the material in the site matches their expectations. Natalie explains how frustrating it can be when the title implies that the site covers one topic and she finds it is actually focused on another:

> . . . [A] good site is when it is like actually on the topic I'm looking up and has a lot of information that I can use on it, and then a bad site is when it . . . leads to something else and then it starts talking about something else—another topic.

She was frustrated that many of the sites she explored for her project on the death penalty had only small amounts of information. One site particularly annoyed her because

> . . . [The Web site] was something on the death penalty, and I didn't see essays or anything on it, and it was just really . . . lots of junk and I was saying, "okayyy." I thought it would be pretty interesting and it wasn't at all.

The site should also be "easy and helpful," according to Kristen. Once she has done a Web search and has selected a site, she does not want to spend more time trying to find the information within the site:

> . . . [T]hose are important things because you don't want to spend hours and hours trying to figure out how to get from one place to another place, so if it's easy and it's accessible, that's good. And if it's straight out helpful, like you can find information and the basic facts, then it's helpful and it's very easy and stuff and you know how to do what comes next, it's good because you don't want to be sitting at a computer forever.

When students go online for information, they expect it to be presented clearly and efficiently. Their purpose for being on the Internet in this case is to retrieve information, not to play endlessly with a computer.

Cityview students know that their keyword searching may lead to extraneous Web sites, but they do not seem quite sure how to refine their searches. Jeff, for example, was frustrated in his efforts to find advertisements for household products from the 1930s. He quickly realized that it would take him hours to go through the list of thousands of Web sites that resulted from his keyword search on "advertising." As he scanned the list, which consisted mostly of Web sites about marketing services, he exclaimed, "I don't want to post advertisements! These people are dumb. . . . I want existing advertisements." Jeff continued to look through the sites for a few more minutes. He did not attempt to narrow his search at all until I suggested to him that he try searching by brand name specific products that were available during that time period.

Another problem is that a single term may produce sites on entirely unrelated topics. Students working on the American Revolution discovered that the names of the historical figures they were studying had also been used for many commercial products. One group of girls found themselves weeding through Web sites produced by the modern-day Samuel Adams brewery when they tried to find information on this early American leader for their social studies project. Similarly, their search on John Hancock led to "all this litigation stuff" (sites relating to a class action suit brought against a major insurance company by the same name). Apparently unaware of the ways in which they could have narrowed their search, the students turned their attention instead to the Battle of Bunker Hill. They were not yet sophisticated enough in their searching skills to eliminate Web sites containing contemporary commercial uses of the person's name by combining the historical figure's name with an event such as the Constitutional Convention or American Revolution.

Cityview students need continued support from their teachers to develop and refine the skills they need to take full advantage of the Internet as an information resource. Online, students encounter a variety of perspectives on any given topic. These students are not yet sophisticated in how they evaluate information and do need assistance in order to construct effective searches, make sound decisions as to which Web sites to use, and discern the subtle biases that may be present in the information. This is not to say that students immediately accept as fact everything on the Internet. Cityview students do recognize that not all the information on Web sites is of equal value. Students see each Web site as the representation of one person or group's understanding. The "author" or designer of the site is a person who is only an email message away. Students take a discriminating approach to online information—in essence, challenging the person associated with the information by comparing it with the information in other sources (both online and print materials) and their prior knowledge of the topic. This is in contrast to students' perception of books, which the teens repeatedly describe as containing "the facts."

Students recognize that anyone can create a Web site and that there is little, if any, control over the quality of online information. They know that there is no review process to prevent the inclusion of biased or inaccurate information on a Web site. The teens assume that it is their own responsibility to filter through the information. Although this can be difficult at times, it is a small price to pay for the freedom that students associate with the Internet. As one student pointed out in an online discussion message[2],

> *Article No. 59: posted by Ducky Big Mouth on Tue, May. 26, 1998, 12:21*
> It seems there is some stuff on the net that is not so important as other stuff. To put in simiply words garbage. But can we truly stop poeple from expressing their idea's . . .

The democratic nature of the Internet affords students the freedom to gather or disseminate their own information on almost any topic imaginable. But Cityview students see the Internet as far more than an electronic library. Searching for information is only one way in which students spend their time online. The technology that expands exponentially the variety and amount of information resources available to students also opens up a whole new world of social opportunities for teens.

Notes

1. On some search engines, these symbols may be used to combine terms in a search, so that the query becomes more targeted.

2. Messages posted by students on the Web-based bulletin board established for this study appear here as they appeared on the computer screen.

7

MEETING THE REAL
PERSON FIRST

STUDENTS' ONLINE RELATIONSHIPS

> If I go online with the purpose of meeting people, then I will
> meet people. . . . [I]f I go anywhere else, you know, like [pause]
> . . . I don't know—in this space-time continuum, there are all of
> these people everywhere, but you'll never be able to meet
> because of the space in between you. But the Internet just for-
> goes that factor of space. That's really amazing.
>
> —Student

Like the indoor shopping malls of the 1970s and 1980s, the Internet
has become a popular meeting place for today's teens. On the Internet,
teens may engage in intimate conversations with a single close friend or in
large public forums with thousands of participants worldwide. Although
some of the Cityview students say their parents liken the Internet to the
telephone, the Internet differs from this earlier technology in that participants do not need to have identified each other prior to their technology-
mediated communication. To use the telephone, a caller must have identified the person to be called in advance, either through a previous
face-to-face contact or the use of a telephone directory. When students go
online, the Internet serves not only as the tool for communication but also
as the means by which the persons to be contacted are identified.

As mentioned in Chapter Five, I discovered the importance of the Internet as a meeting place when I noticed that Cityview students consistently use the pronoun *they* in their discussion of Web sites. In Jeff's description of Web search engines, for example, he points out, "They don't get to look through every page and see what it's about." From an adult perspective, I assumed that Jeff and his classmates are assigning agency or human powers to their Internet-connected computers. One of the ways in which adults have responded to the proliferation of computers in their daily lives over the past two decades is to assign agency to the computer. Unable to comprehend fully the powerful information-processing functions of the new technology, many adults attribute human characteristics and powers to the machine. In a classic example, customers and clients who complain about billing errors are sometimes given the explanation that "the computer did it." Lost in this explanation is any human responsibility for the output of the machine.

At first, I believed that the teens, too, attribute human characteristics to the machine. But as I probed further, I learned that for the students, *they* refers not to the computer itself but to the person or persons responsible for each Web site. For Cityview students, each Web site is a semitransparent medium providing a direct connection to the person who authored or designed the site. Kerri described personal Web sites as a form of conversation:

> . . . [A] lot of people write like they talk. So you can tell on the home pages it was done by one person, cuz they *talk*. If it was done by a lot of people they would've corrected it, over it. But a lot of people on their home pages they talk.

In this way, Web sites are one of the Internet tools with which students connect to others online.

Internet searching technology offers convenient, fast, efficient ways for students to meet others with whom they share common interests. Kristen, although still a beginner on the Internet, is optimistic that she will be able to find chat rooms dedicated to her social studies research topic:

> I've seen people in my um class, have gone into chat rooms to see people's opinions on certain things, which I'll probably do

on this project, because I am doing Amelia Earhart. I was going to use chat rooms for that—to see what people thought of her . . . and so, I'm probably going to use chat rooms for that.

Colin says it is much easier to find friends online than in the traditional ways his parents did (e.g., school social events):

> If I go online with the purpose of meeting people, then I will meet people. . . . [I]f I go anywhere else, you know, like [pause] . . . I don't know—In this space-time continuum, there are all of these people everywhere, but you'll never be able to meet because of the space in between you. But the Internet just forgoes that factor of space. That's really amazing.

These students have discovered that the same powerful Web searching tools that allow students to search for information for social studies or science assignments may also lead to specialized online meeting spaces.

In some ways, going online with the purpose of meeting others is similar to using a dating service. Much is left up to chance when an adult approaches another patron in a popular singles' nightclub. On the other hand, a dating service filters out potential partners with whom the client has little or nothing in common. Similarly, each time a student forms a new acquaintance in a conventional school meeting place, such as the cafeteria, corridor, or playgrounds, there is little or no guarantee that this teen will have anything in common with the other student. The Internet, in contrast, provides teens with an effective means of seeking out others who share their hobbies and interests.

Traditionally, students' relationships are limited by geographical and physical boundaries, such as neighborhoods, schools, and classrooms. A student's interests may be modified as the student negotiates relationships within these physically defined spaces. For example, a child whose favorite game is Monopoly may settle for playing baseball instead because the latter is the preferred pastime of the other children on the street. In school, students often find themselves working on group projects in which they have little or no interest. This can happen even when the teacher allows students to select the topic. Justin, for example, may find that no other students in his class share his deep interest in army tanks. Had he been required to work with a group of classmates for his research project, he most likely would have compromised his interests in order to fit in with the group of students close at hand. The Internet, however, provides students with the communication tools necessary to transcend these geographical and space constraints to learning. Online, Justin has no difficulty locating others who share his enthusiasm for army tanks.

Access to shared information replaces geographical proximity and physical limitations as the enabling factor in the formation of these relationships. Justin included in his Web site links to other army tank Web sites. His hope was that this might lead to a reciprocal action by the designers of those sites and the beginning of an online relationship:

> . . . I wanna have a link to this Web, this tank Web site that I stole my pictures from . . . cuz he has this list of links, so it's a really cool tank site and he talks, like "this is a good site" and so my mission is to get on that list, so I figure if I give a link to his site, he'll put me on the list.

In a classroom with Internet access, there is no longer any need for students to compromise their own learning interests in order to work collaboratively with others.

Jeff and Colin do not need to live in the same neighborhood or even on the same continent as those with whom they play online games. Since only the person's mind moves about the Internet, rides from parents are not needed for friends to congregate online. Colin met one of his best friends, a girl who shares his enthusiasm for a very specific role-playing game, through a Web site:

> . . . But like my friend, she has a very intricate site, she's into . . . Mario RPG. . . . I found [the Web site] has a bunch of different things, and I found it early on because . . . I had just gotten on the Internet and I was thinking about my interests and Mario, so I just put Mario in and I somehow found this. . . . [T]hen I emailed her—I didn't even know it was a her then— and said, "Can I sort of help on your Web site?" . . . and then

she emailed back, "Sure, you can help," and we became really good friends.

A distance of over 1,000 miles physically separates Colin and his friend. Through email and instant messaging, they collaborated to design and maintain a Web site on their favorite RPG.

Similarly, Mark uses Internet technology to share computer files and technical knowledge with friends he has met only online. For Mark, these friends do not displace face-to-face relationships in the classroom. His online relationships provide support for his continued development as a computer expert in a way that face-to-face relationships in the classroom cannot. At school, Mark has already surpassed the technical expertise level of not only his classmates but his teachers as well. The success of these joint projects does not depend on their always being available at the same time. Unlike the telephone, which requires simultaneous use by two parties, Internet communication may be either synchronous or asynchronous. The Cityview boys and their online friends can receive and respond to each other's email messages instantly or at their own convenience. On the Internet, people meet when their thoughts and ideas come together, not when they are both present in the same physical place.

By digitally encoding and preserving each person's thoughts until the intended recipient is available to receive the ideas, the Internet eliminates the time constraints imposed by the synchronous communication in face-to-face or telephone conversations. It no longer matters what time zone the students' friends live in or how much homework they have on a particular night. Students participate in online conversations and projects as best fits their individual schedules. Internet technology, on the one hand, removes time and distance as limiting factors and allows students to communicate with others worldwide. On the other hand, the technology provides the means for the targeted searching that enabled Colin to locate, among the millions of Internet users, another person who shares his enthusiasm for Mario RPGs.

When students go on to the Internet, they leave behind the physical characteristics that play a role in face-to-face communication. Students value the personal safety and freedom they experience in these faceless

Internet relationships. Lynn uses the Internet to commiserate with other girls about boy problems and other pressing personal issues. She described a Web site she and Sarah had used for this purpose:

> LYNN: It was just telling about like—it wasn't exactly giving advice, but it was just sort of like giving—I don't know—like other girls or boys the sensitive boy thing—[laughs; seems like a nervous laugh]. They gave like their own experiences. And it was, like, sometimes when you have nobody to talk to about like bad stuff, you can just go on that home page and be depressed, cuz—[laughs]. . . .
>
> SARAH: It's just like it's the "Are you on the Internet?" guy.
>
> LYNN: No, not be depressed but, I mean—you can know that someone else has the same problem and you're not alone in the world.

The Web site and relationships between participants are defined by the participants' common problems. Unlike traditional settings, in which a student's physical appearance reveals more identifying information than the student would care to convey, the Web site requires a participant to share only the information that person feels is pertinent to the problem to be solved. In this way, the Internet provides students with a safe environment in which to engage in collaborative problem solving on sensitive issues. In this case, the Internet is not a substitute for face-to-face contact; it is a forum for adolescents to discuss topics they would not talk about offline.

Offline, students fear rejection based on their physical appearance. They are more confident that they will be judged fairly by others online where physical appearance is not a factor:

> LYNN: . . . I mean, in real life, if you see someone and they're just—you don't get a good impression of them, then you sort of back away, but on the Internet you can't really tell.
>
> SARAH: Yeah, cuz on the Internet, you meet their personality before you actually—

LYNN: Yeah.

SARAH: —you know, but in real life you see about them—

LYNN: So you get to know them before you get to know that.

INTERVIEWER: It's safer cuz you, you meet their personality first?

LYNN, SARAH, AND CARLA: Yeah, yeah.

SARAH: Yeah, like a lot of people's first impressions are like, "Oh that person's ugly so I don't want to know them."

LYNN: Yeah.

SARAH: Like a lot of people say that, so you meet them first and then like once you meet and you like them—well, like you know them, and then if you see them, you can't be like, "I don't like them any more." Because then that's like . . . no one would say that.

Students seek safety but not anonymity in these faceless relationships. Students want to be known, but they want a direct connection between personalities. Whereas adults may have a need to attach a face to a name in their communication, students growing up with digitally mediated conversations experience online communication as a meeting of the minds. The students view the physical signals in face-to-face conversation as interference and seek to be known apart from their appearance.

The Internet filters out potentially misleading factors, such as facial features, body shape and type, the sound of one's voice, and attire. Students fear that their physical appearance may impede their efforts to let others know who they really are. Colin had already formed a very close friendship with the designer of his favorite RPG Web site by the time he discovered that the person is a girl. As a 13-year-old boy, Colin had not envisioned himself becoming best friends with a girl. At first, the discovery that his online friend was not another boy interfered with their working relationship:

. . . [W]hen I thought it was a guy, I was very, really open, and when I found out it was a girl, I became a little more reserved.

But you know, when we got to know each other a little better, I opened up again. Cuz, well, yeah—in this society, you know, male-female relationships really are just crammed with these sexual things when they don't even need to be . . . even online, that same tension comes up sometimes. . . .

In face-to-face encounters, a person's physical presence influences others' first impressions. Online, students "meet" first and then might choose to "see" each other later. It doesn't matter online if a student is male or female, has a bad case of acne, or is still wearing last year's fashions. Each Internet user becomes known by the information that the person reveals through conversation.

The Internet provides adolescents with safe spaces for continual modification of the identities they wish to convey to others. Online, students can experiment with different aspects of their personalities. Carla, for example, likes to assume an older identity in chat rooms. She and Sarah discussed what they like about these online spaces:

> SARAH: I like going into chat rooms because you can pretend—you can be whoever you want to be. Like you can pretend you're like completely different than you are and no one ever knows that you're lying. . . . Like I could pretend to be like forty years old, but I wouldn't want to do that, but still—[laughs]. Like you could pretend that you're a lot older—
>
> CARLA: You could say like you're 17 or to get people to say hello. . . . I don't lie that much. I just say I'm a little bit older and that my hair—
>
> SARAH: Yeah, sometimes—I usually say I'm a little bit older.
>
> CARLA: —that my hair is longer.
>
> SARAH: Your hair is longer?
>
> CARLA: Yeah, I say *long, long* hair.

Students can experiment with different identities offline, but the individual's physical appearance always provides a link between the different identities. One student who rarely spoke out in class discussion, for example, made frequent contributions to the online discussion for this study. The combination of screen name and faceless online forum allowed the student to experiment beyond the role that teachers and classmates came to expect of him in face-to-face classroom discussion. In contrast, had he suddenly started to speak out more in class, his peers and possibly even the teacher might have been surprised. Since there was no connection between the screen name and his classroom identity, he did not draw unwanted attention to himself when he took advantage of the online setting to depart from his usual classroom role.

Online, students can experiment under different screen names, without clues to connect these identities. Carla entered a chat room as a long-haired 17-year-old and formed a friendship with a male student at a nearby university based on the 17-year-old identity. Although she liked the young man and discovered that several of her friends knew him offline, she became uncomfortable with the age difference and terminated the relationship. Under an assumed screen name, she discovered that she was not ready for a relationship with a man almost 10 years older. She was under no pressure to continue to maintain either the relationship or her 17-year-old identity. She could reenter the same chat room under a different screen name with no physical characteristics to connect her back to the 17-year old identity. On the Internet, she experienced the freedom to learn through this type of experimentation and the personal safety from the potential risks of a 13-year-old's forming an offline relationship with an older man.

The girls recognize that this faceless communication allows people to lie about themselves. Lynn described how they proceed with caution, recognizing from experience that the individual they meet online is only one presentation of the person: "And then, they don't really, they don't know who you are. They don't know anything about you besides just what you're writing down. And so they basically just have to trust you for that." Students maintain that the individual's personality is revealed eventually, even if the person is deliberately deceptive online:

CARLA: And it's not—it's dangerous and it's like good, but it's like—

INTERVIEWER: Dangerous?

CARLA: Cuz you know, like people could say, you know, they could not be lying—they could tell the truth but they could keep stuff because there are a lot of sick people out there, so they could you know seem really nice and stuff and you meet them, but you never know what can happen.

LYNN: Their real personality usually leaks . . . out if you ask them like "what kind of stuff do you like?"

CARLA: It depends how long—

SARAH: But they could be lying about that, too.

CARLA: Yeah, but I mean, eventually—

SARAH: Yeah, eventually you can get to know them.

Carla has received photos from online friends, but Sarah pointed out that even a photograph may not be the "real" person:

CARLA: Yeah, and then like, I met like this kid and like he kept on writing back for two months and he sent me his picture and then like we lost touch.

SARAH: Awww [teasing].

INTERVIEWER: How is that different from like—

CARLA: It's *fun*, though, cuz you don't know this—

SARAH: Cuz you don't know what the person could be like—but he could've sent a picture of like his cousin or something.

CARLA: He was, he's cute!

SARAH: It could've been his cousin.

CARLA: It was Mike, remember that? I brought that picture to school?

SARAH: It could've been his cousin, though.

What might be viewed in traditional offline settings as dishonesty or deception is acceptable in the students' online communication. The absence of a physical presence provides students the opportunity to experiment with multiple identities and, in turn, leads to the students' recognition that their communication is contingent on how each participant chooses to present himself or herself in the particular situation.

Cityview students' online relationships may be very unsettling to adults, who have not grown up with Internet technology. Colin, for example, describes his father's reaction:

> I have a lot of friends online, and some people—well like my father, for instance—he says, you know, "Why would you talk to someone who you can't see and you don't know who they are?"

Although these relationships are technologically mediated, they are still very real to the students. In their Internet use, students have come to expect that they should be able to meet, communicate, and collaborate with their peers worldwide. The Internet allows students to move beyond the time and geographical boundaries associated with face-to-face meetings. Powerful Internet searching tools allow students to be efficient in seeking out potential online friends with whom they share highly specialized interests. Online, students engage in meetings of the minds around shared interests and information. For Internet-savvy students, opportunities for learning embedded in social interaction seem limitless.

Cityview students express neither the need to meet nor the expectation of meeting their online friends in conventional offline settings. Face-to-face contact is not a prerequisite for knowing the individual. In some cases, students prefer not to be "seen," or known by their physical appearance. The Internet screens out any physical features that students feel might cause others to prejudge them and allows students to be known first and foremost by their personalities. The students also enjoy the freedom to choose which aspects of their identities to present in any given online situation. For teachers accustomed to maintaining control of student behavior in the classroom, the faceless nature of Internet relationships raises many questions. Are students likely to behave responsibly in a setting in which no one knows who they "really" are? Even if the teacher trusts the students, what about the millions of strangers out there on the Internet? How vulnerable are the students to online abuse or to exposure to inappropriate materials? In other words, can students be trusted with this powerful new technology?

8

BUT IS IT SAFE?

STUDENTS' ONLINE CONDUCT

Article No 21: [Branch from no. 14] posted by Big Daddy on Fri, May. 15, 1998, 14:29
... I'm sick of all this adults thinking that we're going to "bad" sights. If Adults don't trust us why are the allowing these "bad adult" sights to be on the net at all?!!!![1]
—Student comment in online discussion

As children appear to be outpacing their parents and teachers in computer proficiency, students' online activities and relationships are under constant suspicion. Apprehension surrounding children's Internet use and the ways others might use this new medium to exploit children is expressed in a variety of ways, ranging from popular literature to government policy. In 1983, long before the Internet was accessible to the general public, the cinema movie *WarGames* depicted a teenage computer expert using telecommunications to hack into the United States Department of Defense computer system. As the teen comes perilously close to starting World War III, the movie plays on the worst fears of those who do not thoroughly understand this powerful new technology. More recently, *The Berenstain Bears Lost in Cyberspace,* a book aimed at six- to eight-year-old readers, describes how a group of bear cub students are badly distracted from their schoolwork and even exposed to criminal activity when their school allows them to take home laptop computers (Berenstain & Berenstain, 1999). In the wake of the 1999 fatal shooting and bombing attack on Colorado's Columbine High School, newspaper, radio, and television news reports immediately raised the possibility that the two attackers, both students at the school, had been adversely influenced by the Internet.

In each of these cases, the technology itself, not the user, is vilified. A common adult response to these fears is to attempt to limit children's and teens' access to the Internet. In the *Berenstain Bears* story, the bear cubs' teacher replaces the laptop computers with a school computer lab, the use of which is much easier for the teacher to monitor and control. In 1998, United States Senator John McCain introduced legislation to require all United States schools and libraries to use Internet filtering software in order to maintain eligibility for federal funding. United States President Bill Clinton's response to the Columbine tragedy included a call for greater responsibility on the part of media and Internet industries. A coalition of these industries, in turn, swiftly unveiled GetNetWise, a Web site, which includes safety rules, links to Web sites deemed appropriate for children, and a directory of products designed to limit and/or monitor children's Internet use (International Education Foundation, 1999). Conspicuously absent in public discussion surrounding the regulation of children's Internet use have been the voices of the students themselves.

Cityview students maintain that adults' fear stems from lack of experience with computers. In describing their Internet use, Cityview students differentiate between their own knowledge of the Internet and how they believe their teachers and parents understand this technology. Students believe that not all adults adapt readily to computers. These eighth-graders are sympathetic to the difficulties they feel some of their parents have moving past the technology itself to understand the possibilities presented by the Internet. Jeff described his impatience with his father's focus on the computer itself:

> But my poor dad—he really can't figure it out, cuz like he grew up without computers, and I guess, you know, he can click, but

he wants to do everything so slow and look at everything and it's just like, "dad, go, go, go, go, go, go, go!" but it's probably cuz I'm a kid and he's an adult. . . .

Colin and Justin concurred with Jeff's opinion that the difficulty he believes his father and other adults have is related to their not having grown up with the technology. Jeff explained:

> I grew up in the age of computers . . . like when I was in like fifth grade, we had computers in school . . . and so I got to you know figure out how to click this and click that, and just learn the basics of what—and now I can type pretty fast and I— basically all you have to do is know how to get around a computer and everything else is self explanatory. . . . I mean, it's easier to learn when you're younger. . . . Like we grew up in like a technical age sort of where it's natural for us to look at a screen and move around a little thing, move around a little arrow on the screen.

Jeff compared the daily opportunities he and his friends have to use computers with the special status the technology held when his parents were younger:

> It's not new to us, but when, when [adults] were growing up, computers were like, like large rooms that could calculate one plus one in like a couple of hours, and you know . . . they never get to see these things. . . . They hear about this thing that isn't a human but it can think and it's like a new concept. . . . I do the same stuff they did when they were young, like bike ride and hang out with friends and stuff, but they didn't, they didn't have the choice to have computers and to look at them and to use them for the Internet and stuff and they didn't have that option, so now it's a new thing and it's harder for them to learn, it's just the concept of the thing.

Students see adults as reaching back into their prior experience in an attempt to understand computers. The students themselves have moved past the technical concerns to a whole new world on the Internet. For these students, it is as natural to use a "thinking machine" as it was for their parents to use a typewriter or telephone. Unlike their parents and teachers, the students are growing up with the Internet, where neither the online spaces nor the inhabitants are defined in physical terms. Students are using the "thinking machine" to leave their physical presence behind and travel to spaces in which their relationships and activities are unfettered by physical dimensions.

Cityview students believe that their Internet use is constantly under suspicion. "Adult Internet phobias," a topic first introduced by a student, became a recurring theme in both online discussion and offline student interviews. Students perceive their parents as harboring fears and suspicion about children's Internet use. Students resent what they believe to be a common adult notion that, as soon as students move beyond the reach of their parents by going online, the adolescents lose all sense of right and wrong. In the online discussion, Merlin expresses his belief that adults have extreme notions of the dangers associated with the Internet:

> *Article No 14: [Branch from no. 9] posted by Merlin on Thu, May. 14, 1998, 12:09*
> I think that the Adults are scared because the adults think that their child will do something bad that the [person] who is on the internet will come find you and kil your family.

Merlin was not allowed to use the Internet at home. He said his family had had a computer and an Internet service account for the past year. He cited his mother's concern about possible exposure to inappropriate Web sites as the reason for the Internet prohibition.

Students identified Internet pornography as one of the primary sources of "adult Internet phobias." In their online discussion, students pointed out the irony that adults are responsible for the sites' being on the Internet at all:

> *Article No 21: [Branch from no. 14] posted by Buzz2000 on Fri, May. 15, 1998, 14:29*
> . . . I'm sick of all this adults thinking that we're going to "bad" sights. If Adults don't trust us why are they allowing these "bad adult" sights to be on the net at all?!!!!

Article No 22: [Branch from no. 21] posted by Merlin on Mon, May. 18, 1998, 13:29
Your Right!!! If there are bad adult sights, and the adults don't like it, then why should they be on the net at all? I think that all bad adult sights, should be either deleted or trashed. The people who create these websites are allowing these websites and what if a young child sees these?

Article No 42: [Branch from no. 22] posted by Delia on Tue, May. 19, 1998, 15:02
I totally agree. If the adults don't like it then they should get off. . . .

Students' response when they inadvertently encounter these sites is usually either annoyance or indifference. Jeff explained that Web sites that combine useful information with inappropriate text or images present problems for him when he is working on school projects:

> . . . I found a lot of sites that [the site designers] felt they needed to put something, like you know, uh adult—let's just say "adult" on their pages with all this stuff so I couldn't put links to it because it's you know not for school and you know, it's frustrating, because it's like "Why? Why do you have to?"

When I asked Jeff what he meant by "something adult," he explained further:

> Like naked pictures, or uh, not like, uh, I don't know, just like weird things that are unneeded on the page. They don't really particularly, like, really bother me, but . . . I can't use them for my page. . . . [W]hat am I going to put for my citations? Like, you know, nasty dot com or whatever?

Jeff is not automatically lured into a Web site by naked pictures; rather, he judges a site by its usefulness in relation to the project at hand. The eighth-grade boy feels that he should exclude sites with "adult" material from his project, even if they contain information relevant to his topic. Instead of adding to the site's appeal, the inappropriate images render all the information on the site useless.

On another occasion, Kurt and Marcus were searching the Web for information on jazz musicians to include in a social studies project. Their search for "Duke Ellington" yielded a list of sites on the musician, along with an advertisement for the *Sports Illustrated* annual swimsuit issue, which had just been released a week earlier. Carla, who was seated at the next computer, noticed the full-body photo of a bikini-clad model lying on a beach. Pointing to the photo on the screen, she remarked, "But that's not what we're using the Internet for." Kurt quickly snapped back, "*Sports Illustrated* is all over the place." The boys continued with their searching, paying no attention to the almost nude model. The advertisement fell outside their purpose for being online. Their clicking past it in pursuit of the Duke Ellington information is the online counterpart to a teenager buying a soda in a convenience store, walking past the same issue of *Sports Illustrated* on display at the cash register. Cityview students consistently behave in this way when they encounter sites that might be deemed inappropriate. The teens do not feel they give adults any reason to be suspicious of their online activities and relationships. The students maintain that it is the adults' inexperience with the Internet, not the students' online conduct, that is the source of what students perceive as adult Internet phobias.

Although Cityview students are critical of adult Internet phobias, these teens are far from naive in their approach to Internet safety issues. They know that there are potential dangers involved in their online activities and approach the Internet with caution. Sarah, Carla, and Lynn were wary of providing too much information about themselves online. Sarah mentioned that forming online relationships is safer "if you don't give out anything, like if you don't give out where you live or anything. . . ." Unlike face-to-face meetings, online relationships afford students the safety of being able to disconnect—and, hence, disengage—instantly from any situation that seems in any way threatening. The girls recognize that, by revealing information about their offline identities, they may sacrifice this aspect of online relationships and compromise their own safety.

The girls are very wary about arranging face-to-face meetings with individuals whom they have met on the Internet. Carla explained that, even though several of her offline friends know the young man she met when she posed as a 17-year-old in a chat room, she still believes it would be risky to meet him face-to-face:

CARLA: Oh yeah, [her offline friends] *loved* him. Everyone says Steve's really cool. But like my sister almost got married with a guy. . . . Well, she almost was engaged, but then they broke it off.

LYNN: *Really?*

INTERVIEWER: Was she engaged before she—

CARLA: Oh, no . . . he sent her tickets to meet her somewhere and she went. . . .

SARAH: That's spooky, that's really scary, though. They, they could like—

CARLA: They fell in love and—

SARAH: They could, could like—she—it could have been like—

CARLA: He was too old, though. He was 32 and she was 23.

SARAH: But they, but that's—sorry, I'm like—cuz one of my friends went to meet someone and they didn't show up and she was sitting there for like *hours* and they never came—and when like, they could have come and like—

CARLA: It's a little too dangerous.

SARAH: Yeah, it's like kind of dangerous to go somewhere.

For these girls, there is security inherent in the lack of physical presence in their online relationships. Should they feel threatened in an online relationship, they are only a few keystrokes away from safety. By meeting face-to-face with their online acquaintances, they may sacrifice that safety. In other words, the girls maintain personal safety in their online relationships by restricting their interactions to the Internet.

On the Internet, a user ID and password together serve many of the same functions of a passport. Most Internet service providers, schools, and universities require that each individual enter a unique user ID and password combination at the outset of each Internet work session. In other words, the user ID and password allow a person to cross over the boundary between the offline and online worlds. Once online, an Internet user may need to create an additional ID and password combination for each of many individual Web sites that require users to register with the site prior to their initial use. Carla learned through experience to keep her passwords confidential:

> When I first went online, I gave out my password. It was like so stupid. Like when we first got it, it was that week. So we had to go change it and we went through this whole thing—like my dad's bill went up.

Sarah did not understand the distinction between the ID and password needed to log on to her Internet service provider and the ID and password combinations required by individual Web sites. When she discovered that she needed to supply an ID and a password to enter the Web site for a popular teen magazine, she was reluctant to pursue the task any further:

> SARAH: . . . [W]hen you go to a thing and they ask you your password when you sign up and someone told me you're not supposed to use your password any time ever, so should you still give your password?
>
> INTERVIEWER: Your password?
>
> SARAH: Like your password to get on the . . . Internet. Someone told me, like—
>
> LYNN: Your user name?
>
> SARAH: No . . . when you first hook on, you have to type in your password and someone told me never to use that and they asked for it—when you're signing up for other places.

Until I clarified for Sarah that this Web site was asking her to create a password and an ID specific to that site, she had assumed that she needed to enter her Internet service password and ID. Unlike Carla, Sarah knew that she should not reveal this ID and password combination to anyone. As appealing as the magazine Web site was, Sarah chose not to use it rather than to provide an ID and a password that she knew should be kept confidential.

Sarah and Carla are intrigued by the convenience of online shopping for popular teen products, including clothing and music CDs. Carla explained that, although she can go to the mall or a catalog for these items, online ". . . it seems *easier*, okay! No, cuz like instead of looking through the catalog and writing it out and sending it in . . . When Lynn and Sarah interrupted and laughed at Carla's idea of the Internet being the easiest way to order, Carla conceded that the phone is also an option, but she still prefers shopping online. According to Carla, her parents ". . . just think [the Internet's] a waste of money and paper and all that stuff," but her older sisters use the Internet for "everything," including reservations for a recent trip to Jamaica. Sarah wants to shop on the Internet for music CDs but is worried about supplying her home address and a credit card number in online transactions. As enthusiastic as Carla is about the Internet, she shares Sarah's concerns. Lynn explained, however, that there are certain conditions under which these transactions may be safe. She uses factors such as the size and name recognition of the company to decide whether or not it might be reliable for online purchases.

During the months that I spent at Cityview School, online shopping was in its infancy. Reports were just beginning to surface that vendors were using highly sophisticated Web-based technology to collect consumer data from unwitting Internet users. None of the students indicated any awareness of the fact that by shopping online they become passive suppliers of their personal interests and buying habits to Internet-based marketing firms. But Cityview students were very cautious about actively supplying online any information that might provide a link between their online and offline identities.

The potential for misuse of information on the Internet extends beyond credit cards and user IDs. Widespread Internet use has raised many new questions regarding intellectual property rights. The extent to which copyright law applies to online documents has been debated from the United States Congress to law school classrooms. College faculty and secondary school teachers worry about the ease with which students can plagiarize information obtained on the Internet. At a number of Web sites, students can obtain instantly and at little or no cost entire research papers on typical school topics. Students can also cut and paste text and visual information from almost any Web site into their own print and electronic documents.

Cityview students maintain that the collaborative nature of the Internet complicates the concept of ownership rights to online information. On the Web, traditional lines of ownership are blurred as Internet users constantly create new combinations of information in their Web sites. Rickie had difficulty with this when he incorporated a variety of perspectives in his Web site on the assassination of President Kennedy:

> . . . I just put mostly just facts. Sometimes I put little like opinions, but mostly I put facts and I tried to be careful with like plagiarism, cuz that's—like [the teacher] said I plagiarized too many people . . . you know, I sort of disagree with him, but I just try to get all the facts down. . . .

In creating a Web site, Rickie not only encountered many diverse theories on the Kennedy assassination; he also became engaged in the complex question of what constitutes plagiarism on the Internet. Although Rickie continued to disagree with the teacher on where to draw this line, he was careful to follow the teacher's guidelines in his research paper and Web site.

The question of who holds the rights to visual images on the Internet proved particularly problematic for students. Colin and Jeff pointed out to Justin that he really shouldn't provide a link from his Web site on tanks to another Web site from which he "stole" pictures:

COLIN: No, but I mean, you shouldn't make a link to a page you stole pictures from . . . That's like saying . . . "This is the bank that I stole the money from. I stole it on this day."

JEFF [SARCASTICALLY, PRETENDING TO BE THE DISCOVERED BANK ROBBER]: This is really odd, because they caught me, you know. . . .

COLIN: [Laughs.]

JUSTIN [REFERRING BACK TO THE OWNERS OF THE TANK PICTURES]: They won't notice—[pause, voice sounds tentative and unsure of this].

I asked the boys to explain further how they determine who owns the pictures and when they might be stealing online information:

INTERVIEWER: How do you get around—you said you "stole pictures from," all right? How—I mean there's so many millions of thousands of pictures out there on the Web and then when you open up a book, there's all those pictures there . . . . How would you do it so they are really and truly your pictures?

JEFF: You have to go to a graphics place and draw your own—

COLIN: Truly *your* pictures? Well, if you want them photographs, you have to take the photographs yourself. Or you get an art program and you draw stuff. Like I have a bunch of friends that draw their own graphics and give them to friends. Like there's this one kid and his screen name is Slimu, and he had this one style where he gives his pictures to all his friends' Web sites. That's how you'd make them your pictures. But I think *hardly* anyone out there actually has *their* pictures on their Web site.

In describing his own Web site, Colin explained that it is important to acknowledge the sources of all the items he uses, even those which he includes purely for the purpose of entertaining visitors to his site:

. . . I was just surfing around the Web pages one day, and I saw this, this picture of this, this woman in this karate position and this Japanese flag in the background and I said, "Hey, Justin, check this out!" And he said, "Hey, you should get that and say it's your girlfriend." [Laughs, then shifts to mock of very low, serious tone of voice.] So I have pictures of my girlfriend—don't tell my parents. . . . I don't think that counts as information, but I put links to those pages anyway, because I borrowed quote—unquote information from them so I at least want to give them some credit.

The Cityview students who designed their own Web sites recognized that, as Internet users copy visual images and text from one Web site to another, original ownership of the image becomes difficult to establish. What is important to the students is not the individual image itself, but the unique combination of text and images that makes up any given Web site. Still, as Colin indicated, the students do see a need to credit others wherever possible.

Not all information shared on the Internet is beneficial to computer users. The safety concern students express most frequently is the threat of computer viruses. A computer virus is a code hidden within a program. The virus has the potential to damage or destroy other programs on a computer when the infected program is activated. A virus can spread from one computer to another as files are exchanged online among Internet users. A virus is not only a technical problem; it is the online version of a personal injury:

COLIN: . . . Sometimes the Internet can be the equivalent of a street corner in the bad part of town, you know. [Laughs.]

INTERVIEWER: Should you be there? [Asks with quizzical facial expression and tone of voice, so as not to be judgmental.]

COLIN: [Laughs.] Well, there are a lot of—yeah, yeah.

INTERVIEWER: How is [using the Internet] different from standing out on—I mean, like—I mean, if my kid ever told me she was going to stand out on the corner of [name of nearby street in a neighborhood considered to be dangerous]—[laughs].

COLIN: [Laughs.] Well, you can't get shot, um or mugged or anything—there always is the, the ever-present problem of viruses, of you know . . . . In my naiveté when I was . . . an unexperienced user, I did download a . . . virus and that was very scary, because every time we logged on, it would send an email to somewhere . . . with our email address and our password. Yeah, fortunately, we got [virus protection software] and we got that cleaned up.

Whereas a mugging may leave a person with physical injuries, a virus limits a person's ability to participate on the Internet. In the worst case, an Internet user ceases to exist in the online spaces if the person cannot log on. Mark's computer was completely disabled by a virus attached to a file he received from an online friend:

. . . What happened to me last time is I got this program and it erased a lot of my computer's files and it probably had a virus, so I had to reinstall my Windows 95 and like a lot of things got erased. . . .

Until he was able to reinstall his computer's operating system and pro-grams, Mark was unable to engage in any of his usual online activities or relationships.

The students' fear of viruses has no counterpart offline and has grown out of the students' online experiences. Similarly, preventive measures taken by students are designed specifically for the online spaces. Mark described the steps he takes to avoid viruses:

MARK: Well now I have a virus detector, so before I, I download it, but it's zipped—do you know what that is?

INTERVIEWER: Yeah.

MARK: And before I unzip it or anything, I check it for viruses.

INTERVIEWER: What virus software are you using?

MARK: Um, [names two popular virus protection software programs], cuz that, that has, um, detects a lot of . . . viruses.

INTERVIEWER: . . . So, like, when, when somebody does that to you, like when somebody sent that to you, how do you respond? Like, do you just never talk to the person again, or do you—

MARK: Well, I got hold of him and I said, "Why'd you do it?" And he said he didn't know it had a virus and somebody even sent it to him and nothing happened on his computer, but then I reported him [to the Internet service provider], cuz you go to this section where you could report people that send like email attachments or send you um just messages, and so I—he didn't know I did that, but I did it.

Viruses have no physical dimensions. Still, they loom as a serious threat to students who have become fluent Internet users. As Mark and Colin became more experienced on the Internet, they learned basic safety precautions to guard against this danger. These precautions—using antivirus software, checking downloaded files for viruses, and reporting the source of any virus detected to the Internet service provider—are routines students develop specifically to meet their online safety needs. In this way, students' sense of the risks and dangers on the Internet and the precautions they take to avoid these hazards are grounded in students' online experience.

Cityview students' Internet use extends well beyond the exchange of information. These students rely heavily on Internet communication tools as a convenient and efficient way to meet and form relationships with their peers worldwide. Students value the direct contact between personalities they experience on the Internet, but also they recognize that it leaves students open to personal hurt. Colin discovered this vulnerability when another Internet user responded to his Web site:

If you make a page . . . you're putting yourself out there . . . and I think that you're putting yourself, all of you out there for people to look at you and think you're cool or to IM [instant message] you and say, "you suck" [lowers voice]. But, that's happened to me a couple of times, but let's not get into that.

Colin, in turn, found himself in a situation in which he had the potential to hurt an online friend when he discovered that one of his "really good friends" was a girl and not a boy, as he had assumed:

> . . . [T]his person Weevil, I didn't know. I assumed that she was male. I find that I sometimes—I just assume the person I'm talking to is like me in gender and in age, and I'm sure trying to get past that, but—

Long after Colin had become friends with Weevil, he discovered that she did not meet his criteria for offline friendships. He was faced with the choice of rejecting Weevil on the grounds that she was a girl or revising his concept of friendship to fit the faceless nature of Internet relationships. At 13 years old, Colin chose to get past his prejudices, rather than to hurt someone he had never actually seen before and could instantly cut out of his life by discontinuing his online communication with her.

On the Internet, the students take their responsibility as participants in online communities very seriously. The rules that help to delineate the boundaries for each space are negotiated by the participants. Early in the online (Web-based) discussion set up for this study, a student using the screen name Schoolman720 posted a message that referred to another participant by the second student's offline name and associated him with the stereotypical computer hacker:

> *Article No 9: posted by Schoolman720 on Tue, May. 12, 1998, 16:27*
> I have a question for you guys: why do you think some adults (I'm not saying any names) are SO SCARED of using the Internet, or letting us? I mean, do they think we're dumb enough to get instructions for a bomb and blow our heads off? Or are they just scared of change, and maybe still getting over this new-fangled MI-CRO-WAVE O-VEN thing? Perhaps they think someone like [Trek618's offline name] is going to hack into our computer, learn everything down to when we go to the bathroom, and come kill us. (You hacker-people can't really do that, can you [Trek618's offline name]?? HUH???) Or maybe they're just dumb! What do you think?

Article No 15: [Branch from no. 9] posted by Trek618 on Thu, May. 14, 1998, 12:53

Mentioning such names in this way can be hurtful to others. Next time be careful what you say!!! I don't know sqwat 'bout the dang-fangled INTERNET 'N' SUCH. the only thing I do know is how to search for websites. P.C. usage is different! that's what I do know! and HACKING is not just breaking into computers and files!!! it is also re-configuring programs (this is where I specialize)!!!!!

P.S.

Schoolman720 who ever you are . . . just be careful next time!!!!!!!!!!!

Article No 19: [Branch from no. 15] posted by Schoolman720 on Fri, May. 15, 1998, 10:55

Look, sorry man! I was just trying to make a point, and demonstrate your adeptness in computers. I didn't mean to be hurtful. . . . I'm sorry. . . . Please forgive me. . . . ::sobs::

Trek618 never returned to this online space to hear Schoolman720's apology. After his apology, Schoolman720 continued to read messages but never posted another one. In Internet terms, Trek618 had stormed out of this room, and Schoolman720 retreated into a corner of the online space.

The use of screen names provided anonymity for the author of each message. Neither the school's Internet use policy nor the online discussion guidelines based on this policy accounted for the possibility that a participant would refer to another student by offline name in the text of a message. This incident set off a string of messages regarding acceptable conduct on this site:

Article No 23: [Branch from no. 19] posted by Merlin on Mon, May. 18, 1998, 13:30

Who are u and what did I say? Did I say something bad?

Article No 29: [Branch from no. 23] posted by DD33 on Tue, May. 19, 1998, 08:36
I just think that all u people r really crazy!

Article No 47: [Branch from no. 23] posted by Bo on Wed, May. 20, 1998, 16:56
Stop playing on this site

Article No 58: [Branch from no. 47] posted by Zena16 on Tue, May. 19, 1998, 08:34
I agree to not play around on this site, but if someone is trying to make a point to others about something that is said in this internet discussion, I think they should say it. That doesn't mean being disrespectful to one another though.

These messages were interspersed throughout the students' continued discussion of adult Internet phobias—as previously discussed, the label students give to what they perceive to be adult suspicion of students' Internet use.

A brief message I posted to suggest that students not use offline names was ignored by students as they continued to negotiate among themselves the boundaries of this particular online space. Two teachers were assigned accounts, so that they could monitor the discussion for compliance with the school's conduct code and Internet use policy. They did not return to the site after the first week. Adult involvement was reduced to the researcher's responsibility for maintaining the technical aspects of the Web site on which the discussion took place as students themselves maintained acceptable conduct for the discussion. In their messages to each other, the students defined this online space as one in which participants respect each other and tolerate diverse viewpoints.

Cityview students have encountered the assumption that there is something deficient about their online relationships. Colin said that he has been criticized for his online relationships both by his father and

". . . [O]ther people, like my one friend. . . She says, you know, 'you have friends online. I'm sorry but that is really sad.' " The students' standards for acceptable conduct in the online spaces indicate that the students using the Internet are doing something more than sitting in front of a computer terminal. Electronic images on a screen would not command the level of respect students expect of each other online. Students recognize their online friends and acquaintances as real persons, requiring at least as much respect as would another student standing in front of them in the classroom. The faceless nature of students' Internet relationships is not to be confused with anonymity, which is often associated with an accompanying lack of responsibility for one's actions. As participants in online communities, students establish a code of conduct to account for the personal nature of online communication and are quick to correct each other for behavior that, either intentionally or unintentionally, may be offensive or hurtful to others.

Cityview students are savvy in their approach to Internet safety. They have identified a variety of risks associated with Internet use, ranging from potential credit card misuse to disrespect for personal feelings. Through their Internet use, the students have developed precautions that, like the problems themselves, are grounded in their online world. These teens contend that adult Internet phobias stem from adults' lack of experience in online relationships and activities. This raises the question of whether or not the students will volunteer to share their experience and serve as guides for teachers trying to navigate this strange new online world.

Notes

1. As mentioned in Chapter Six, messages posted by students on the Web-based bulletin board established for this study appear here as they appeared on the computer screen.

9

THE INTERNET
GENERATION IN SCHOOL

Using Technology in the Classroom

. . . Netscape is becoming that—their [the students'] electronic
library.

—Teacher

. . . [I]t wasn't really using the Internet, no. I do really use the
Internet [outside school] for other things.

—Student

A common assumption surrounding young computer users is that,
even without formal instruction, Internet-Age children and teens
quickly become technical experts. As part of its marketing campaign
for computer training programs, Compaq issued a two-page advertisement featuring a futuristic photo of a young teen sporting several wear-
able computers. The caption read "Right, like I'm going to teach him
about computers?" The advertisement urged teachers to enroll in the
company's computer education program, "so you can teach your kids
with confidence. Instead of the other way around." For generations,
schools have operated on the assumption that the teacher possesses
knowledge that is vital for students to master and that it is the teacher's

role to impart that knowledge to students. As the advertisement suggested, the proliferation of computers in schools and the ease with which children seem to adapt to the new technology present a potential role reversal. Unlike professionals in most other fields, teachers are surrounded all day by cyber-savvy youth. These students, who are using the Internet regularly on their own, could help their teachers to keep pace with this rapidly changing technology. The proliferation of computers in schools, combined with the ease with which students seem to adapt to computers, poses a new question: will students share what they know about the Internet with their teachers without an explicit invitation to do so?

Cityview School, as a result of careful planning and wise spending, faced this question earlier than most schools. In 1994, Cityview embarked on a long-term planning process, which resulted in a 10-year vision for the school. By 1997, the school had an Internet-connected computer to student ratio of one to six. According to one of the teachers who participated in the planning process, the school's leadership ". . . felt that computer technology, primarily the Internet, would be an invaluable educational tool, particularly for the economically disadvantaged inner city kid." The Internet, according to this teacher, would provide the opportunity to

> . . . get our kids out in a way that would not require them physically to be in the space. It would open up to them lots of opportunities. And, it would open up to the teachers lots of new tools to use in the classroom beyond word processing.

The school moved quickly and, within two years, raised enough money to wire the building and equip each classroom with three computers, all of which are connected to the Internet.

At Cityview, the Internet is utilized more as a tool within the classroom than as a vehicle to "get out" into other spaces. When one teacher elaborated on how he expected to see the Internet used on a day-to-day basis, he made an analogy to calculators to point out that teachers, not the technology, are in charge:

. . . [I]f I would ask that question about the calculators . . . then I would be thinking about there may be days when it is not being used at all because it is not a tool to get at what my objective is in the instruction. I don't want my kids using calculators to do 20 × 6. . . . But if they're going to be doing something that is extensive, they may use a calculator or they might be using it for an entire hour if this big project is going on and there's a lot of number crunching. . . . I'd be adverse to saying . . . "an hour of a kid's day, or 10% of a kid's day, or 15% of a kid's day is going to be spent on a computer, because . . . then my curriculum is being driven by use of the technology. . . . I would rather just think about, what are my curriculum objectives and how does this become a tool for the kids. . . .

In his comparison between calculators and the Internet, the teacher defines the Internet as a tool that is easily controlled and contained within the classroom.

Cityview teachers view the role of the Internet in the curriculum as an information resource for student research projects. The school's Internet use policy refers to the school network (which connects classroom computers to the Internet) as a means to "conduct research and communicate with others" (see Appendix A, "Cityview School Acceptable Internet Use Policy). In describing their expectations for students' classroom Internet use, teachers focus on research, with the Internet serving as a substitute for or an extension of the library. Although Cityview's Internet policy makes provisions for student email use, teachers have not indicated that they expect students to use Internet communication from the classroom.

One teacher uses the Internet as "a really important essential tool, . . . the other major point of access to ideas and information" in the absence of a school library.[1] In another class, students use the Internet before and after visits to the neighborhood public library. Students use the public library's online catalog to select the books they need before they leave the classroom. If students return from the library with insufficient information for their projects, the teacher refers them to the

Internet as a supplemental information source: the teacher believes that ". . . it is a real blessing that we have the software to do this . . . because [there is not] a really good reference library in this school anywhere and so Netscape is becoming that—[the students'] electronic library."

The school's technology plan is based on the same principle that shapes Cityview's use of school library books, according to one teacher:

> . . . [I]t's always been Cityview's thinking whether it's comput-
> ers or library resources or audio/visual equipment, that rather
> than having them centralized in one space, like the library, a
> computer lab or an AV closet, that they are in the places where
> they will get the most use and where they have, they are, of
> greatest accessibility to the kids and the teachers and that is in
> the classrooms. So, we made a very conscious and deliberate
> decision, years ago, to have a library in every classroom and
> that's perfect for the students. And we made a conscious deci-
> sion to have computers in every classroom so that they are
> accessible and can be integrated.

Though inconsistent with the seemingly random nature of the Internet, the library metaphor lends shape to the Internet that teachers can relate to a pre-Internet institution defined in part by physical dimensions. Unlike the vast, constantly changing information resources available on the Internet, a traditional print library collection, prior to the intro-duction of digital technology, was finite, organized, and ordered. Cityview teachers expect students to use the Internet as a tool to gather information, in the same way they might use an encyclopedia or a library book collection.

In school, students rarely use the Internet for any purpose other than gathering information for assignments and projects. Colin is quick to point out that the Web searching he did for a group research project on local architecture was not really using the Internet:

> Well, sure, we uh we used Yahoo. We put in, we typed in dif-
> ferent names of house styles or parts, names of parts of houses
> and it brought up a bunch of sites with useful pictures on it. . . .

> That's the extent that we used Internet for that, for that one. . . .
> It wasn't really using the Internet, no. I do really use the Inter-
> net for other things.

Two teachers referred to this same project as a model of exemplary
Internet use by the students.

Colin was skeptical of how adults, myself included, understand the
Internet. He asked me if I define the Internet as "the concept of being
online or the World Wide Web." I explained that I am interested in any
Internet functions he and his classmates use. Colin then added that searching the Web for project information is only one of the ways in which he
uses the Internet. "I do have [Internet service]," he pointed out, "and I use
email and instant messages and I go into chat rooms and I often go on the
Web so sometimes for school things . . . other things too."

In school, Colin and his classmates confine their Internet use to
Web searching. Colin utilizes the other functions that he mentioned in
the 90% (Colin's estimate) of his Internet use that occurs outside the
classroom and is not school-related. At no time do students challenge
their teachers to go beyond using the Internet as a delivery system that
brings information into the classroom and to move out into the online
spaces students know from their out-of-school Internet use. Rather
than point out to teachers that the Internet is more than an electronic
library, Colin and his classmates go along with their teachers' definition
in the classroom and wait until off-school hours to use the Internet as
a vehicle for communication.

Teachers express concern that searching the Internet may not be the
most efficient way for students to get information. As much as the
Cityview faculty see the need for students to use computer technology,
the Internet as an electronic library is still subordinate to the traditional
print resources, such as books and periodicals:

> It's not that I don't want [the students]—I mean there is some-
> thing very attractive about using it. . . . You can kind of sense
> it. I find personally it takes so long. I just think it is difficult to
> get information as quickly off the Net as I do in the library.

In contrast, students repeatedly describe the Internet as being a much more convenient source of information than a library constructed of bricks and mortar. Kerri described trying to find a particular book during a recent visit to the public library to illustrate why she prefers the Web:

> And I just, my eyes were like crossing at the end of that and I was getting really frustrated cuz I couldn't find [the book she needed]. . . . My teacher came by and was like, "Kerri, what are you doing?!" And I was like, "I can't, can't find the book." . . . [W]hen they say that the book is at a location and I know that this specific book I'm going in for, but it's when they have it *all mangled up* in the library. Like women's rights will have battered, rape, . . . *all these books!* . . . [S]ome of the books, they would have women's rights and they wouldn't have anything about voting, which is the first thing you learn. . . .

Kerri compared the difficulty she had locating information on women's suffrage in the library to her experience searching the Web for the same topic:

> . . . I like the Web, because it gives you what you *really* want. . . . I can just go in specifically to what I want and I don't have to read *all* this to find out on the last page, "Oh, this is what I wanted!" And it's easy, cuz you can just browse in and browse out and turn the page and . . . you only print out what you want. You don't have to print out the amount of a book, which is like two hundred pages and what you needed is in the middle, so you can read the *whole* book to find out. . . .

The same Internet searching technology that allows students to identify potential friends among millions of Internet users can be used to obtain information on very specific topics. In the library, a student has to search through a catalog (either online or a paper card catalog), identify a book on the assigned topic, find the book on the shelf, and then locate the pages with pertinent information within the book. Web searching, in contrast, is like one-stop shopping. A student with basic searching skills can use Web search engines to ferret out precisely the information needed and then view, print, or save to a disk that information without ever leaving the computer workstation.

In school, the Cityview students honor their teachers' preference for print materials. In the research papers for their eighth-grade mastery projects, students relied heavily on print resources, including books, newspapers, and magazines. The bibliographies of 30 student papers listed 180 print resources and 36 Web sites. Only one student used more Web sites than print items. A paper on the history of computers listed no Web sites in the bibliography. The student who authored this paper had used as the starting point for his project the detailed timeline on the Boston Computer Museum's Web site. A student who was observed incorporating information from a wide variety of Web sites on the assassination of President Kennedy into his own Web page on this topic listed only one site in his research paper bibliography.

Students maintain that the Web is a valuable information resource and at the same time honor the value their teachers place on print materials. Students made several trips to the public library in order to get the print materials required for their mastery projects. Two students who I had observed relying heavily on Web resources omitted Web sites entirely from their bibliographies. Bibliographic information for many of the omitted sites was readily available. These two students bookmarked sites on classroom computers and included links to selected sites in their own Web pages. In their mastery project research, students went along with what they perceived to be their teachers' emphasis on traditional print resources. Students accepted the inconvenience of using the library (relative to accessing the Internet from the classroom) or did not indicate the degree to which they had relied on the Web.

When students use the Web as an information source, they are exposed to a wide variety of multimedia presentations. Internet technology allows for the instantaneous transmission of information in text, still visual, audio, and video formats. For example, Web sites on President Kennedy's assassination include countless photos and graphics demonstrating the possibility of a second gunman. On Web sites dedicated to contemporary music, students can listen to samples of music from compact discs newly released by their favorite music stars. The combination of media and hyper-links makes the Web "magical" and fun for Cityview students. In their research for school projects, however, they set aside the information presented in multimedia formats. With the exception of the Web page design, a special project limited to six participants, students focus on the text mode historically emphasized in school.

Kerri, for example, described how she is strongly attracted to the visual aspects of Web sites but disciplines herself to adhere to the text-based learning expected in school. Her first criterion for selecting a Web site from a list of sites generated by a search on her topic is ". . . if there's bright pictures, stuff that's like really graphic, stands out, catchy." As she works on her school projects, she sets aside her interest in visually attractive Web sites for those that are dominated by text:

> . . . I go to some really boring sites and they're really—I think the most, the most . . . the Web sites that give me the most information are the ones with all the texts. I have to find myself saying, "Okay, Kerri, look for text, *not* pictures, *texts*."

Kerri's understanding of the mastery project research paper was that pictures could be included as a supplement to—not a substitute for—text:

> . . . I could put [a picture] in the middle of my research paper, but um, what's bad about it is I have to make sure it *is* five pages . . . a minimum of five pages, because if it's not, it would be too short. Cuz I have to make sure, okay, this space [motions with hands a length of space about two inches long], I have to count this space, and say, "Okay, I have to add, say this much space to the five pages cuz I took them out to use for a picture or something."

Kerri explained that the mastery project consists of distinct components, ranging from a research paper to an art project. (She did not include the Web pictures in her art project because they did not fit the focus of the assignment.) Kerri's interpretation of the mastery project is that text is the legitimate form of information in school and that pictures are best left for the art project. She believes her preference for Web sites that effectively combine visual and textual information does not meet her teachers' expectations. Kerri, often outspoken in the classroom, responds by restricting herself to text-based learning, not bothering to include pictures in her report. She sets aside the way she learns best and goes along with the written presentation that predominates in secondary school classrooms.

Even when students do use multimedia tools to represent their own learning, the projects are considered supplemental to conventional research papers. During the final quarter of the year, Cityview eighth-graders completed an interdisciplinary project on a topic related to the theme of "change." This was the one class assignment for which the students' classroom Internet use extended beyond using the Web as an electronic library. Included in the five project components were a research paper and an art project. Six boys chose to design Web pages on their research topic, one of the options for meeting the art requirement. This project, which teachers limited to six students to match the number of computers available in the two eighth-grade classrooms, was the only time I observed students using the Internet in the classroom for any purpose other than Web searching. As a student project, Web page design raised questions regarding assumed classroom practices.

For his Web page, each student gathered information from a variety of books and Web sites, selected the information he felt was most important to convey, and decided on the balance of "fact" and "opinion" to include in his own site. Colin explained how he as a Web site designer combined his own thoughts with other information he found online:

> . . . [F]or my uh page, I have you know, the links to these 12 other pages where they have a description of the different astrological signs, and you know, for the like actual adjectives and descriptions I got from other places but—like ambitious emotional and stuff—but I wrote it all and I shaped it into a you know, a structure and the places that I got it from I quoted them and I even put links to places to order the books and stuff. . . .

At the same time, the students decided how to integrate text, pictures, and links to related Web sites for the best presentation of their topics. When asked how they selected what to include in their pages, the students cited a variety of criteria:

ANDY: Just examples from other Web pages—

JUSTIN: Yeah.

ANDY:—like how something looks, puttin' a picture here, a picture there, some text there and—

JEFF: I just have fun with it.

JUSTIN: I just find basically what I hate about all other Web pages and don't include that and what I wish they had and put that in there.

Each student wrote original text for his site using information gathered from both online and offline sources. Simultaneously, the students used computer cut-and-paste tools to add in pictures and links to other sites to complement the text. Students were in agreement that, by the time they submitted the Web pages for grades, they had spent far more time on this project than they would have on a paper or another offline project.

None of these students questioned the fact that the teachers had organized the mastery project so that their Web pages counted only as the art project, not as a substitute for the research paper. Although the students agreed that they preferred this project to a conventional research paper, the Web page was not a less demanding option for students hoping to avoid a writing assignment. The boys estimated that they invested far more time in constructing projects in this format than they would have on a paper or another offline class project. The students favored the Web format over a paper because it gave them the "freedom" to demonstrate "creativity, originality" and "more personality" in how they conveyed information on their topics. The students found the Web page to be a highly motivational and dynamic project open to continual revision. The boys did not, however, raise the possibility that the research paper may be an outmoded format and that Web page design provides the opportunity to learn the online multimedia publication skills needed for the 21st century workplace. Instead, the students went along with their teachers' emphasis on text-based learning and submitted without question text-only research papers as the core component of their mastery projects.

Student-designed Web pages raise new issues in relation to grades, which constitute a defining element of the teacher-student relationship. Typically, grades are used to motivate students to master the material that the teacher expects them to learn. No matter how much a student learns in a school year, a good grade is contingent upon demonstrating the knowledge and skills that the teacher deems important. Teachers at Cityview have discovered that the range of information readily available on the Internet poses a dilemma for teachers. What students study is no longer limited by the textbooks housed in the school. When the Internet is available in the classroom, students have convenient access to the information resources to pursue almost any question or problem that occurs to them. This raises many questions about who decides what is important for students to learn—the teacher or the students.

The first year Cityview School had Internet access, students were allowed to choose their own topics for a Web page project. One teacher became frustrated by what he described as students spending "an incredibly ridiculous amount of time" searching the Web for backgrounds and other features to copy into their own Web sites. After this experience, he felt obliged to direct student learning toward the topics and skills teachers feel are most important for students to know:

> Hopefully, by actually making them do research and consider what is of value to know and learn, I think that would be a better use of the Internet than [getting a] background with Mickey Mouse or look at the Disney site for three days.

For the 1998 mastery project, teachers provided a list of suggested research questions from which students could choose their topic. Students based their mastery projects on these or closely related questions.

Whereas some students were highly engaged in their topics, others were less enthusiastic. One girl said that she had selected weather as the best topic left when she returned to school after having been out sick on the day project topics were chosen.

The long-established practice of grading assumes that the teacher possesses knowledge about the topic and or skills desired. At Cityview, the range of Web page topics was more controlled in 1998 than in the prior year, but the teachers were still faced with assessing a new product with which they have had little previous experience. When asked how they expected their Web sites to be graded, the students designing Web pages expressed uncertainty and apprehension:

> JEFF: That's what I'm wondering. . . . I'm scared that [the teacher is] going to be like "well, you didn't do this, so you failed!". . . . He never gave us a clear description of what we're supposed to do so he just said sort of like you know "Go off with this and make your Web pages," so when he comes and evaluates us and if he gives me a bad grade . . . there's really nothing I can do, cuz—or he probably shouldn't be able to because he never gave us expectations.

> ANDY: I think that he probably grades us on like accurate information and like graphics and like the way it looks and all the stuff in it. I guess.

> COLIN: . . . I was thinking about this the other day and the good thing about this particular medium, you know, the Web page, is that this is all new to [the teacher] and pretty much *anything* we put on there, he's gonna be impressed with . . . I'm not saying that to get away with anything—but I think that we're gonna get a good grade, you know.

> JEFF: . . . I didn't put too much info; I put more like you know cool little pictures and like linking things. . . . I figured this was sort of an art project instead of a display our information project. . . . I mean, hopefully that's what he's looking for and not what [the teacher] doesn't want to happen. . . .

JUSTIN: . . . I just tried to be really creative with mine, come up with some new ideas that I had never seen before, like putting hidden messages and stuff like that, because I figure he'll think that that's pretty creative and . . . give me a good grade.

None of the students indicated that they had asked the teacher for grading criteria for the project.

Later in the conversation, the students explained how they would grade the Web pages if they were teachers. Jeff made a distinction between the types of projects that might culminate in a Web page and was very clear in his assessment criteria for each:

Okay, if it was for a research project, I'd grade it on like the information they have and how well they displayed it and how easy it is to read and stuff. And if it was an art project, I'd grade them on their creativity . . . how the page layout is and how interesting it is and stuff—how colorful, magical, happy.

The students did not mention the paradox that part of the teacher's role is to grade this project even though the students believed they themselves were far more experienced Web users. Instead of questioning the teacher's ability to grade the projects, the students guessed at what the teacher was "looking for" and what they were "supposed" to do. Students thought they knew more than their teachers about Web pages but went along with the customary expectations for teachers and students. The students perpetuated the recitation model by speculating about what the teacher's expectations might be and then attempting to provide the right answer in their Web pages.

The students' understanding of curricular expectations is not the only factor that limits the range of Internet functions these teens use in school. When using classroom computers, the students face technical obstacles as a result of measures taken by the school to ensure network security. Features built into Cityview's computer network, for example, prevent students from using audio and video materials that are available on the Web and should be easy and convenient to use. On one Web site, for example, a student can click on a photo of a famous jazz musician to see a digital video of a historic performance. Unlike video-tape, which requires a VCR and monitor, multimedia clips in digital form can be played on the computer the student is already using to connect to the Internet. A multimedia Web site may, however, prompt the student to follow on-screen directions to download a "plug-in," a specialized computer program required to play the digital audio or video clips.

While Mark and Sean were researching 1930's radio programs, they discovered that they needed to download a "plug-in" program called Real Player in order to listen to old-time radio songs available on the Web. Mark quickly realized that the school's network security program, which guards against hacking and viruses by preventing unauthorized access to the school's network, also prohibits students from downloading plug-ins into student file space on the network server. He devised an alternative plan to download Real Player into the teacher's directory and then move the program files into his own directory.

When Sean approached the teacher and asked for help with this strategy, the teacher responded, "Can I just put in my password?" After the teacher typed in the password, Mark attempted again to download the files. He then quickly scanned the teacher's directory of files listed on the screen to locate Real Player. After he found the necessary files, he proceeded to complete the registration and installation process that should have enabled him and Sean to listen to the 1930's songs. Mark typed in the teacher's and school's name along with his own email address (obtained through the Internet service provider he uses at home) and moved the files over to his own student directory. The screen immediately displayed a network message indicating that he did not "have enough privileges" on the network to run this application. "Oh my god," he responded. He named another teacher and mumbled, "Like she probably put in a password protected thingy on [the network security program] so we can't play it. She's so overprotective." Half an hour after they had first located the 1930's songs, Sean asked, "Why don't you put it on your [floppy] disk?" Mark responded, "I already have this program at home." The boys agreed that they should abandon the project for the time being and that Mark would tape songs from his home computer onto a tape cassette.

Mark did not question the teacher he believed was being "overprotective." Even though Mark uses the same type of multimedia program outside school, he offered a number of minor logistical problems as reasons his approach would not have worked:

> Um, well, we tried to get some actual music from the computer, but it didn't work because I had to be in the teacher's [computer account] and it was too much work asking for the password each time, and even if I didn't get a—I'd have to get a recorder and record it right from the computer, and it wouldn't be, it wouldn't be, it was kind of loud in the class, so it wouldn't really pick up anyways.

By finding fault in his original plan and devising the solution of tape recording songs from his home computer, Mark avoided the possibility that he knows more than his teachers about the Internet. In the excuses and explanations students offer for their teachers, the students honor the teacher's role as dispenser of knowledge. Even in this highly student-centered school, students choose not to acknowledge that they know more than their teachers about the Internet and, instead, maintain a relatively passive role when it comes to classroom technology use. In school, Cityview students set aside the alternative strategies for using the Internet that they have derived from their own experience in using the technology. Preserving the teacher-student relationship to which they are accustomed takes precedence over maximizing the use of the Internet.

Downloading multimedia files is not the only task complicated by school security measures; even working with Web-based text files is difficult for students at times. Cityview's network security rules prevent students from taking full advantage of their home computers for school assignments. Jeff explained why he does not use floppy disks to bring to school information from Internet searches he does at home:

> INTERVIEWER: So you look for information—and then do you print it out? Do you save it on a disk?
>
> JEFF: I—we're not allowed to bring disks from home to here because of viruses, but—but no, I just print it out.

INTERVIEWER: Is that a classroom rule or school?

JEFF: School rule.

INTERVIEWER: So you have to print it out, and what do you do with it when you bring it in here?

JEFF: I either type it back up or—that's pretty much all I do, I just type it back up.

INTERVIEWER: So—okay, you're printing it out, but you can't, you can't move anything back and forth on disk?

JEFF: No, it's, um, it's stupid. They have a virus scanner, so you figure why, why are they gonna care, but, being safe, I guess. . . .

Jeff does not protest the school rule regarding floppy disks, even though he and other students have learned through experience how to protect their home computers from viruses. Instead, he does what he needs to—in this case, printing at home and then retyping at school all the information—to get along within school rules. Any challenge to the rule would contradict one of the most fundamental assumptions on which school as an institution is founded, that in the classroom "teacher knows best." Jeff's retyping of online documents demonstrates the lengths to which students will go before suggesting that they know a better way to use the technology than do their teachers.

Security concerns extend to cover the use of Internet communication functions, which Cityview students rarely use in school. The school's Internet use policy does not prohibit Internet use for communication and includes guidelines for student email use. (See Appendix A, "Cityview School Acceptable Internet Use Policy.") Teachers are aware of a commercial Web site that provides free email accounts and were considering taking advantage of this service for their students. Their decision was stalled, according to one teacher, because the school had not yet worked out a procedure for monitoring student email:

What we are trying to do is to work out a situation where we have control over that which will allow each student to have an account with their own password. And we are trying to work out the things as to how we control what they send and what they receive. . . . But we are in that discussion. . . . As you know, there are so many things out there that they could potentially get into. Not only addresses that are not for their age group, but also messages that they could send to people that aren't really the people they're dealing with and you don't know what is going on out there. That's what we are concerned about.

When describing the school's long-range goal of providing each student with a laptop computer and home connection to the Internet, another teacher spoke of teacher-centered email use:

. . . [W]e even at one point were thinking about trying to get some funding to put a laptop in the hands of every kid, . . . so the beginning in fourth grade your house was modemed and then—because our teachers give out their phone numbers . . . they are answering questions about homework and sometimes they're on the phone, depending upon what you assign, for a good hour or two—and can the technology enhance that? . . . On Saturday morning from ten to eleven, any questions you're having about the project you're doing this weekend, let's get it out. There's more emailing. You know, having email accounts for everybody to kind of go back and forth. And I think those types of things would be interesting to think about.

Internet communication, including email and chat rooms, falls outside the dominant classroom pattern, in which communication flows primarily through the teacher. When students use email from classroom computers, teachers no longer control when, where, or with whom the students talk. Efforts to monitor all student email, in effect, maintain pre-Internet control of classroom communication.

On two occasions, students familiar with Web sites that provide free email attempted to send messages from classroom computers. Jeff became frustrated that the designer of a particular Web site had not kept the site current. He took advantage of the email box built into the Web site for user feedback to remind the designer that the site should be either maintained or removed from the Web. Weeks later, he said that he had not yet received a response, but he did not expect one. There was no email box at school for him to receive a return message.

Mark tried to email a project file from a school computer to his home computer, so that he could work on the project outside school hours. He went to a Web site that provides free email and set up an account for himself. He then sent a message with the project file attached from this new account to the commercial email account he uses outside school. Mark's creative solution to the problem of moving a file too large for a floppy disk failed. He speculated that the project file might have been larger than the free email service permitted.

Other students know how they could have used Internet communication in the classroom. Colin described how he would have used email to send specific questions on his mastery project to the designer of the Web site he (Colin) had used most. Kerri and Kristen speculated that they might have participated in chat rooms focused on their research topics but did not because chat rooms are forbidden in school. Neither girl has consistent access to the Internet outside school. None of these students is critical of Cityview teachers for not providing student email accounts and chat room access. The students are indifferent in their descriptions of their proposed purposes for and failed attempts to use these functions, as though they have no expectation of using Internet communication in school. Students wait until after-school hours to use the Internet to connect with others beyond the walls of the classroom. Pre-Internet patterns of classroom communication remain intact.

The Web pages designed by the six boys who chose this option for their mastery projects represented another opportunity for student communication to extend well beyond the classroom. When a Web page is made available on the Internet, it becomes a vehicle of communication between the designer and the user. A page becomes accessible to other Internet users when it is stored on a server that is connected to the Internet. A server is a computer designated to provide, or "serve," data to a network. It was unclear from interviews and observations how well students designing Web pages for their mastery projects understood the technical process by which the Web pages become accessible to others on the Internet. These students did, however, expect that a wider audience beyond the classroom would use their pages.

As the students worked on the pages, they frequently referred to the other Internet users who they expected would use these Web pages. Colin and Justin both built "hidden" features into their Web pages to amuse users. These cartoons appeared only if a user clicked on the right spot on the Web page background. Colin worked diligently to figure out how to add an email function to his page, so that users could send feedback to the email address he used at home. The students engaged in serious conversation about how another Web page designer might respond to seeing tank pictures from his Web site on Justin's page. Contrary to students' expectations at the outset of the project, however, the pages were not made available to Internet users outside the school.

On two occasions, a teacher said that the pages would be available on the Internet. The students had no reason to doubt the teacher; a Web site designed by students in the prior year in partnership with a nearby university was already available on the Internet through the Cityview server. As the end of the year drew near, another teacher referred to vague technical problems that might prevent storage of the six student Web pages on the school server. As students were nearing the completion of the pages, they questioned whether or not the pages would be put on the Web:

COLIN: Wait, are these Web sites going to be like available to everyone?

ANDY: No, just people from the school.

COLIN: Cuz if they are, I better take my full name off of there. . . .

ANDY: No, it's probably just the school.

COLIN: I hope they do, but I doubt they'll be able to—

JUSTIN: They probably won't.

COLIN: —but it would be pretty cool if they did.

JEFF: I hope they do, but I doubt if they'll be able to.

INTERVIEWER: Why do you say you doubt they'll be able to?

JEFF: Because, because, I don't know—I think you need to pay money to have the page on the Web and I think you need to have the computer on all the time if you do.

COLIN: Well, you could put it on a free place, like [name of commercial Internet service that provides free server space for Web pages].

JEFF: Yeah, actually I'd like to do that!

INTERVIEWER: Um hm?

JUSTIN: Because—

JEFF: That'd be awesome if I could have my own page.

JUSTIN: —last year I know they put everyone's page on the Web. . . .

The Web pages, which represented eight weeks of student work, were not transferred to the school server and could be accessed only from the specific classroom computer on which each student had designed his page. The possibility for students to share their projects with and receive feedback from other Internet users worldwide was lost.

Students did not complain. Instead, they offered cost and technical problems, such as needing to keep a computer on all the time, as explanations for why their teachers had not put their work out to be viewed and critiqued by a wider audience. None of the students raised the possibility that the teachers did not know how to get the pages onto the Web. Students could not take on this task because the network security program barred them from installing files on the school's network server. After eight weeks of intense effort on their projects, the students passively accepted that their projects would not be communicated to a global online audience. Too large for students to save on floppy disks, the Web pages were left behind on classroom computers at the end of the year.

These teens do not anticipate that the scope of their classroom Internet use will change soon. They recognize that they have had a unique opportunity at Cityview, where the technical capacity (hardware, software, and network) far exceeds that of other area schools. Most Cityview students expect to use the Internet for school-related projects far less as they move on to various high schools. Lori's prediction for her high school Internet use is typical of the views expressed by her classmates:

> . . . [A] lot of the work that we're gonna be doing, I don't think I'm going to be using, needing the Internet for them. I think we're going to be using a lot of books and not computers and things, so I don't think I'm going to be using it as much as I used it at Cityview.

The Internet, according to Daryn, ". . . is more of a middle school thing. . . . It's just more like a—a fun activity" that has no place in the serious work of high school.

Jeff is an exception. He anticipates that he will use the Internet much more heavily next year. He differs from his classmates in his assumption that high school teachers place more emphasis on content and exercise less control over how students conduct their research than do Cityview teachers. He expects to be using the Internet "a lot more" in high school

> . . . cuz [high school teachers] give you specific topics. . . . [T]hen you go on the Internet and find out about those topics. Here it's more broad and general . . . and we have guidelines for like what to research, cuz we're sorta learning how to research here, but once we get into high school, it's going to be like "go find out about this" so I'm going to use the Internet a lot more.

Jeff believes that Cityview teachers' purpose in specifying the number of books and Web sites students must use in each project is to help students learn how to do research. In middle school, he goes along with the requirement to use a variety of formats (e.g., book, periodical, Web page). He expects to rely much more heavily on the Web in high school, where he believes students themselves will be responsible for determining what formats to use.[2] Jeff described an anticipated increase only in the volume of his school-related Internet use, not in the range of Internet functions he will use in the classroom. Using the Web to gather information for research projects is the only function he mentioned in this conversation.

None of the students expressed any expectation that they might use the Internet as a communication tool in the classroom. Students give no indication that they see themselves as having an active role in determining how they use the Internet in the classroom. With the exception of Jeff, students assume that their future classroom Internet use will be determined by their teachers' understanding of the technology as an information-gathering tool, not by the students' own experience using the Internet as a dynamic combination of information and communication functions.

In school, Cityview students do not live up to the popular expectation that cyber-savvy students will lead the way in classroom use of 21st century technology. Instead, two critical patterns have emerged from the comparison between what the students know they can do with the Internet and how they use the technology in the classroom. First, the only Internet function these students use in school is the Web. In their classroom, the students rarely use the Internet communication functions they depend on to participate in online relationships and activities outside school. Second, students do not question either implicit or explicit limits on their classroom Internet use. The students do not voluntarily step out of what they understand to be their place in the classroom in order to show teachers new ways to use computers. Students maintain a passive role in classroom learning decisions by honoring their teachers' understanding of the Internet, even though the students believe they know more than their teachers do about the Internet. The teens' understanding of their role as students takes precedence over any influence that their out-of-school technology use might have had as a catalyst for fundamental change in classroom learning. Given the students' reluctance to step out of their understood role and teach their teachers about the Internet, schools need to develop effective professional development strategies to help teachers keep pace with their students' Internet use.

Notes

1. Cityview School does not have a centralized school library staffed by a library media specialist. Some teachers indicate that the school has no library; others refer to the book collections housed

in individual classrooms as the "school library." Teachers and students rely heavily on a nearby public library for research purposes.

2. *Format* is not to be confused with *source* in this context. *Format* refers to the particular medium by which the information is conveyed. *Source* refers to the supplier of the information. A student may use Web pages as the only format and have 10 sources—that is, information from 10 Web pages, each authored and designed by a different person or organization.

10

CATCHING UP TO KIDS
What Schools Can Do

. . . [T]here's not too many times that teachers in the school [are] on the computers. Very rare that I find them on the computers.

—Student

Over the past two decades, schools have struggled to meet the high cost of computer hardware, software, and networking. One of the most pressing concerns for teachers is that the high cost of these tangible items leaves little funding for the professional development they need to understand better how to use the computers in their teaching. Where professional development is available, the typical approach is to address the integration of technology into the classroom as the first step. In other words, professional development is based on the assumption that teachers will be motivated to use technology in the classroom because it is somehow beneficial to students growing up in the 21st century. What is missing is a convincing response to the question that teachers need answered: "What is in it for me?" The end result, as Cityview students have experienced, is that, even in a school that both teachers and students recognize as being advanced in its classroom technology use, Internet use falls far short of what the students know to be its potential. Although Cityview faculty require the students to use the Internet for their research papers, students are not convinced that their teachers either embrace the technology or fully understand its potential uses.

In their classroom Internet use, Cityview students experience incongruities between their online learning and established classroom practices ranging from time allocation to assessment. Web-based learning, which allows a student to pursue an interest to the depth that satisfies the adolescent's curiosity, for example, may not coincide with established grading periods. The opportunity to forge learning relationships that extend beyond traditional boundaries of time and place conflict with the model of the classroom as a closed communication system in which the teacher controls when and with whom students talk. What the students have discovered is that the Internet as they experience it does not fit *into* the classroom, yet the focus of most professional development for teachers is on integrating this technology into the classroom as it currently exists. Instead, teachers need to approach the Internet as a vehicle for venturing out into new learning environments that may be far different from anything in their prior experience. An alternative strategy to professional development is to provide teachers the support they need to become learners first—then teachers—with the Internet. In this way, instead of fitting the Internet into the classroom, teachers and students together can build connections between online and classroom learning.

Students themselves are a critical untapped resource in this approach. Although many adults view students who are growing up with computers as natural or expert Internet users, students will not voluntarily share what they know with their teachers. When the Internet was introduced into Cityview School classrooms, neither the teachers nor the students automatically abandoned the roles associated with a traditional teacher-student relationship. Long before reaching eighth grade, these teens learned—not necessarily at Cityview—that success in school depends on figuring out what the teacher is "looking for" and then providing the right answer. Even though Cityview is known for its progressive, student-centered approach to learning, students using the

Internet persist in patterns of interaction associated with the traditional notion of the student as recipient of knowledge imparted by the teacher. In school, students set aside their understanding of the Internet as an integrated communication and information system and work within their teachers' understanding of the technology as an information-delivery system, or electronic library. In other words, the students do not see it as their place in school to show their teachers how to use the new technology, even though the students believe they know more about the Internet than do their teachers. In acquiescing to their teachers' expectations for classroom Internet use, Cityview students leave to the faculty full responsibility for identifying and implementing any changes in student learning that might accompany this innovation in the classroom.

In their out-of-school Internet use, Cityview students experience learning as a messy, sometimes inefficient process that is not compatible with the day-to-day classroom routines that evolved long before the invention of the Internet. On their own, Cityview students use the Internet to engage in constructivist learning, in which they constantly revise their understanding of any given problem to reflect the new perspectives and information they encounter online. Online, students learn that there is no single right answer to any given problem. As they follow links through the web of information available online, students discover their learning outcomes to be variable, multifaceted, and unpredictable. Students find that there is far more information conveniently available to them on the Internet than that for which the teacher or curriculum planner has accounted. For prior generations, the teacher was the primary source of information beyond that which children learned at home. In the Internet Age, the teacher is only one of many experts accessible to students, as Web pages, email, and chat rooms provide children and teens with countless convenient opportunities for direct communication with specialists in any field.

If used this way in the classroom, the Internet calls into question the underlying assumption on which the teacher-student relationship is based: that students look to the teacher for knowledge they need and to which they do not otherwise have access. Any revision of the teacher's role to account for students' Internet use calls for a simultaneous reconsideration of the student's role. The teacher alone cannot effect change in the student-teacher relationship, any more than one partner in a marriage can change how that relationship functions without active participation by the spouse. The classroom teacher cannot take on the role of coach or facilitator unless students understand that they are expected to take a more active role in decisions surrounding their learning. It is not enough for teachers and school administrators to share a vision for change in classroom teaching and learning; expectations for how student learning will change must be made explicitly and repeatedly clear to students.

The introduction of the Internet into the classroom may be used to begin a dialogue among teachers and students about the students' role in decisions surrounding their learning. Renegotiation of the relationship between teacher and student to account for student Internet use implies active engagement of the students, as well as the teacher, in the conversation. Even at Cityview, a school that places exceptional emphasis on student involvement in the learning process, students show little indication that they would initiate or enter into this type of discussion on their own. Very early on in their schooling, students grow accustomed to having learning decisions made for them by teachers. Teachers will need to take responsibility for engaging students as partners in this change process.

From the perspective of their students, however, teachers lack the credibility as Internet users that the teachers need to enter into this conversation. A paradox then arises: teachers need to invite their cyber-savvy students to enter into conversations about how their Internet use impacts classroom learning, but the students do not believe that the adults around them fully understand what it means to work and play online. The students honor their teachers' authority within the context of the classroom, but the traditional grounds for that authority—the teacher's role as dispenser of knowledge—have changed. Students know they can use the Internet to bypass the teacher and gain access to vast amounts of information and experts on almost any topic. The students maintain that they know more about using this technology than do their teachers but do not volunteer to share their expertise with teachers.

Given this paradox, teachers are faced with two options. The first is to continue to function within the existing classroom structure and routines. In this instance, both the topics studied and the learning strategies used in school may become increasingly irrelevant to students as they take advantage of Internet access outside school to learn about their own interests. As with the Cityview student who is developing into an online technical support expert, the students' independent online learning may be highly valuable but still not coincide with the curriculum. Similarly, although students know that they can email project-related questions to the authors of Web sites on these topics, the students set aside this strategy in favor of compliance with school prohibitions on Internet communication. In these and many other instances, students perceive adults in their school as lacking understanding of the Internet. Students observe teachers either not using the Internet at all or using it only as an information-delivery system. Students know from their own experience that school use of the Internet as an electronic library falls far short of the possibilities presented by the technology when it is used as an integrated communication and information system.

A second option is for teachers to become online learners along with their students. Teens, long recognized as experts, or naturals, with computer technology, have the potential to play an active role in any change process that might follow the introduction of the Internet into the classroom. But by adolescence, students have learned well their place in school and are unlikely to initiate the role reversal necessary for them to share with their teachers what they know about life on the Internet. School administrators and teachers must be highly proactive in any effort to include students in meaningful conversation about how to bridge the gap between the classroom and the online learning environment that these teens experience in their out-of-school Internet use. A necessary first step is for teachers to establish credibility with the students. With increased experience online, teachers may abandon efforts to confine Internet technology to the classroom and grow comfortable with the concept of venturing out into online spaces the way their students do.

Just as it would be ill-advised for a teacher to use a textbook or videotape without previewing it, teachers should not be expected to guide students through this new online territory without first exploring it themselves. The critical difference between the Internet and the media previously used in the classroom, however, is that it is impossible to preview or even predict all that is now instantly available online. Both the information available and the opportunities for communication with other Internet users are constantly changing and expanding. This is in sharp contrast to the traditional instructional model, in which the teacher is expected to maintain control over both classroom communication and the range of information to which students have access. Given the nature of the Internet as the students understand it, the focus for teachers' professional development needs to shift from *what* is available online to *how* to live and learn in this new environment. In other words, teachers need to experience for themselves processes such as pursuing learning needs indefinitely through a massive Web of information, forming online working relationships, and negotiating and self-monitoring rules of conduct in spaces with no physical dimensions. Obviously, it is impossible for teachers or anyone else to know all that is possible on the Internet, but, the more familiar teachers become with working and playing in this new environment, the more credibility they will have with their Internet-Age students. This shared learning experience then forms the common ground for teachers and students to renegotiate classroom relationships, so that the teacher serves as coach or facilitator as students take fuller responsibility for their learning.

One difference in how Cityview students use the Internet outside school and what they believe their teachers expect in school is that the students' out-of-school use is free of curricular assumptions about what is most important to learn and the best way to learn it. Students find that learning on the Internet is limited only by their interest in the topic. Neither the availability of resources in the student's immediate physical surroundings nor the teacher's knowledge of the topic is relevant to the scope and depth of knowledge the student can pursue on the Internet. As understood by these students, a curriculum based on predetermined outcomes is an artificial construct that is contrary to the messy, unpredictable learning they experience in their out-of-school Internet use. Students need to see indications that their teachers have experienced the type of learning that results from following pressing concerns through a Web of online information and communication with others interested in the same topic. For adult Internet users, topics may range from pressing medical concerns to favorite recreational activities. One teacher, for example, mentioned that he found the Internet very useful in planning a recent vacation. Since his home access was slow and inefficient, however, his primary experience was limited to using school computers to gather model lesson plans.

Cityview students recognize each Web site as the representation of one person or group's understanding. Given access to multiple resources, their learning becomes a process of constantly evaluating information and revising their own understanding. As a result of their online learning, students in this setting understand that there are a variety of strategies for solving and representing any given problem. Although Cityview teachers encourage students to consider multiple perspectives in the combination of print and Web resources required for their research projects, students still attempt to predict and provide that which they believe their teachers expect in the final project. Kerri, for example, omitted all pictures from her research paper because she believed her teachers did not value visual information. Similarly, Jeff attempted to provide in his Web site the elements that he thought the teacher was looking for.

For kids growing up with the Internet, static learning resources, such as textbooks, supplemental library books, newspapers, and magazines, no longer suffice. These students expect to be able to pursue their interests indefinitely through a vast web of information. They understand that their pursuit of knowledge around a certain interest may lead them off into other unanticipated topics. They consider dialogue with others who share their interests to be a critical part of the learning process. Students need to feel that this type of learning is not only sanctioned but actively supported in school, so that their in-school learning begins to correspond more closely with the learning they experience as they move fluidly between online and offline spaces.

Classroom Internet access presents the opportunity for teachers to model for students online problem-solving strategies that depend on diverse perspectives represented in a range of formats. As students discover in their online learning, links to additional information often lead in unanticipated directions, requiring constant revision and refinement of the topic studied. If students see teachers learning this way, the students may further abandon the idea that there is one right way of doing things in school. Their own learning experience becomes a critical guide as students develop strategies for researching and representing any given topic. Students' ability to assess the effectiveness of any given problem-solving strategy may, in turn, become a higher priority to students in their classroom learning.

Cityview teachers may already be using the Internet in this way outside school, but students do not believe that their teachers are fluent Internet users. One student commented that, whereas students use the computers "every single day" in the classroom, "there's not too many times that teachers in the school [are] on the computers. Very rare that I find them on the computers." On a daily basis, students need to see teachers engaged in online learning that mirrors the students' experience with the Internet as an integrated communication and information technology. It may then become easier for teachers and students together to use the technology to support a continued shift in the emphasis of classroom learning from content to process. The use of the Internet to support this shift—a change Cityview is already moving toward in its project-based curriculum—may give classroom learning greater relevance for students. In addition, the teacher is freed from the expectation of requiring a right answer or a single best problem-solving strategy, expectations that students still maintain in their understanding of classroom processes. At the same time, students may feel less of a need to figure out what it is the teacher wants or expects and can focus instead on continual development and assessment of the processes by which students construct their own understanding.

Students believe that adult Internet phobias form a significant barrier, which prevents their teachers from moving beyond using the Internet as an electronic library to fully experiencing online learning. For Cityview students, the value of the Internet as a learning tool lies in the opportunity for online communication around shared information on any topic. Students maintain that school restrictions on Internet communication result from adults' suspicion of students' online relationships.

The students believe that this fear stems from the teachers' own lack of experience with a full range of Internet functions. If this assessment is accurate, one way for teachers to establish credibility with students is to gain and demonstrate experience in online relationships. These experiences might range from using email to obtain information from specialists on a topic of personal interest to joining teachers and students from other schools in online collaborative projects. Teachers may already be cultivating their own networks of online friends and colleagues; however, students report seeing little evidence of this in the classroom.

Cityview students learn through their online relationships that the Internet is not an unruly frontier. Teachers may be less hesitant to integrate Internet communication into classroom learning if they themselves participate in the process of negotiating and then self-policing rules for online spaces. Students demonstrated this skill and responsibility in the online discussion they participated in as part of this study. As with any other school policy, there is no guarantee against the occasional abuse of Internet communication privileges by individual students. However, understanding, as students do, that participants in each online space maintain an expected code of conduct may help teachers to find a middle ground between reading every student email message and prohibiting students from using email at all. Students experienced at negotiating rules in online spaces are an important resource in the establishment of consequences for students who violate the school's expectations for acceptable conduct on the Internet. Teachers may also discover that various Internet communication devices, such as email and chat rooms, are not intrinsically detrimental to students; the value of each technology as a learning tool is dependent on its use. As one Cityview student pointed out, for example, chat rooms are subject-specific, with topics ranging from "intellectual" to "entertainment."

Cityview students acknowledge that the information and individuals they encounter online may present risks, but they also believe that the benefits of online communication far outweigh the potential dangers. Students understand that the Internet can be, in one student's words, ". . . the equivalent of a street corner in the bad part of town . . ." and develop safety routines to protect themselves online. In school, students experience limitations on their Internet use, which they believe would not be necessary if their teachers were to share the students' understanding of online safety routines. This is not to say that students believe that they should be allowed to use the Internet with no supervision; rather, teachers' guidelines for school use would have more credibility for students if the teens believed that the guidelines were grounded in teachers' online experience, not in adult Internet phobias. One of the ways in which students know what precautions to take, for example, is by knowing what pranks they can play online. As one girl pointed out, students maintain a healthy skepticism in their online relationships, since they know that they, too, can misrepresent themselves in the faceless online environment.

The faceless nature of Internet communication is conducive to teachers' shifting to the role of learner. Cityview students value the personal safety and freedom of the faceless Internet relationships, which allow them to experiment with various aspects of their personalities. Online, teachers have the same freedom to experiment that their students do. On the Internet, everyone is a potential teacher. In online communication, individuals assume the role of teacher or learner, according to the expertise each brings to the problem at hand. This allows a teacher to avoid any assumptions of superior knowledge associated with his or her role in the classroom and to become a learner; as the teacher pursues learning on topics of high personal interest, no one can connect the teacher back to the offline professional position. Teachers may set aside lesson planning in their discipline to practice online learning around any topic, regardless of the teacher's prior knowledge of that subject. Unlike the classroom where the teacher is expected to have specific plans for moving students through the curriculum, on the Internet a teacher can participate in online conversations and follow links from site to site without knowing what will happen next. Teachers can even go into the game rooms and teen idol Web sites popular among students without anyone knowing that they are teachers offline. If teachers use the Internet the way their students do, the technology can be both a space for teachers to experiment in their own learning and a window into their students' world.

Teachers need to be given the same freedom the students have in their online learning. Instead of focusing on how to use Internet resources in the science or social studies curriculum, initial professional development for teachers should be aimed at encouraging teachers to pursue their most urgent personal learning needs first. Although the Internet has great value as an electronic library, this is only a starting point. In order to learn other ways to connect classroom and online learning, teachers must be encouraged to approach the Internet in the same way their students do—as explorers in a whole new world. Rather than adapting a pre-Internet understanding of what and how students should learn in the classroom to the online environment, teachers need to discover new ways of learning made possible by this innovation. Just as the automobile allows drivers to explore new territory far beyond that which was previously logistically sound to consider, the Internet provides teachers and students together the opportunity to delve into new learning opportunities not yet imagined.

If teachers embark on careers in education at least in part because they enjoy learning, they should be ideally suited to taking an exploratory approach with this new technology. But they cannot do this without substantial support from their schools. Students have already discovered that learning in this new environment may not always fit the routines that have evolved to promote efficiency in the classroom. Cityview students discover and participate in their most constructive online learning outside school. Teachers, too, may experience more freedom as online learners if they are encouraged to use the Internet for their own learning needs outside school. If teachers are fluent Internet users themselves before they take on the task of integrating the technology into their teaching, they may be better able to envision new ways of classroom learning to keep pace with students' out-of-school Internet experience. One way for Cityview to support teachers as Internet users is to provide them with adequate computer hardware and software, Internet service, technical support, and training to use this technology consistently outside school and to encourage teachers to use it for their own learning purposes before they start using it in conjunction with their teaching. This may help to address an incongruity that Cityview students recognize: teachers are expected to guide students in learning with a cognitive tool that was not part of the teachers' own experience as students.

Obviously, it is not realistic for most schools to provide every teacher with the computer and Internet service necessary for home Internet access. There are, however, a number of strategies that might be used as incentives for teachers to participate in online learning beyond the already overcrowded schedule of their school day. Teachers can buy computers at significantly discounted prices if they are given the option to participate in bulk purchases as the school or district orders computers for the schools. Low-interest loans and payroll deduction plans make the initial computer purchase more feasible for many teachers. Even if cost is not a barrier, many new computer users are daunted by the task of shopping for a computer. Comparison shopping is impossible if the new computer user does not understand the terminology used to describe the features and capabilities of the machine. Any professional development program for teachers new to computers should include information on how to purchase a computer. Newspaper, magazine, and Web site advertisements for computers may be used to help teachers understand the terminology associated with computers and to identify which machines best meet their needs and budgets.

The purchase of a home computer does not automatically remove all barriers to teachers' out-of-school Internet use. Teachers may also need assistance in understanding how to select an Internet service provider. A common mistake made by new computer owners is to default to an Internet service whose software is factory-loaded onto the machine, even though this service may not be the best match for the person's needs. Monthly fees for Internet service may also be prohibitive. Some of the more creative school districts and universities in the United States are funding their own Internet costs by establishing the district or institution as an Internet service provider and selling low-cost Internet service to local residents. Technical support is another problem; although computers are rapidly taking on the status of one more household appliance, reliable service technicians are still in short supply. Vocational programs aimed at students interested in pursuing careers as computer technicians can provide students with real-life experience and can offer a valuable service to the school community by establishing an on-campus computer service shop. Telephone technical support is another service that these students could provide, again gaining work experience in the process.

This is not to say that professional development designed to assist teachers in using the Internet in the classroom should be eliminated; rather, curriculum applications should not be the first Internet use teachers encounter. As long as teachers are introduced to the Internet within the context of classroom teaching, the possibility of maximizing the technology as a support for constructivist learning remains limited. The classroom as a social organization predates and does not account for the new learning opportunities afforded by this innovation. If teachers first become fluent and versatile Internet users outside the context of classroom instruction, they may bring to subsequent professional development a greater ability to rethink classroom processes to account for students' online learning. Professional development can then effectively foster joint consideration of classroom learning and the opportunities presented by the Internet, so that new learning goals emerge that were not possible prior to the introduction of this technology into the classroom.

This professional development approach, which could prove most effective over the long term, may not appear efficient within the context of the immediate, day-to-day pressures on classroom teachers. Schools are under constant pressure to integrate computer technology use into student learning. Scarce professional development time and dollars are allocated toward familiarizing teachers with curricular applications of the new technology. Teachers learn about ways that their students can use classroom computers, but the teachers' own learning needs are neglected in the process. The idea of "doing it for the kids" goes only so far for overworked teachers; at some point, they need to know how using the Internet benefits them. Even if teachers do not voice this question, it needs to be answered. Otherwise, the technology use will fall by the wayside as teachers encounter the inevitable obstacles to day-to-day classroom computer use.

Instead of jumping immediately to teaching with technology, the initial focus of professional development for teachers needs to shift back to learning with technology. This approach requires schools to take a step back before moving forward, but at this point there is little to lose. Too many classrooms are already cluttered with underutilized computers, which fuels the argument that Internet technology is only a distraction from the "basics" assumed to be most important for students to learn. Given that the integration of technology use into student learning lags well behind school acquisition of hardware, software, and Internet connections, a new approach to professional development is called for. Addressing teachers' own learning needs first will help teachers to gain confidence in working with their cyber-savvy students. Teachers will gain the credibility as online learners that Cityview students currently believe is lacking. In addition, if teachers value the Internet in their own personal learning, they may be more likely to forge past the many obstacles to school technology use in order to work together with students to connect classroom and Internet learning.

The Internet, in the words of one Cityview teacher, ". . . really does seem to be the wave of [the students'] future." Teachers are left with the choice of either becoming increasingly irrelevant in how they present knowledge to their students or renegotiating with students the teacher-student relationship and classroom routines derived from this relationship to account for students' online learning. Before students will invest in this conversation, they need to see their teachers as experienced and versatile Internet users. If teachers become fluent online learners, the students may be more likely to share their visions for learning in what one student predicts will soon become a "more Internet-oriented world."

CITYVIEW SCHOOL ACCEPTABLE INTERNET USE POLICY

The Cityview School recognizes that telecommunications and new technologies have altered traditional ways of communicating, transferring, and accessing information. We are supporting access by students to these rich information resources. The school intends to teach appropriate skills to analyze and evaluate such new resources.

EDUCATION is the primary objective of using telecommunications at Cityview School. Students use the network to conduct research and communicate with others. Students are responsible for good behavior on school computer networks. General school rules for behavior and computer use apply. Access to networks is provided to students who agree to act in a considerate and responsible manner. The use of telecommunications at Cityview School is a privilege not a right which may be taken away from students who do not follow the rules and regulations.

All Cityview School students will be expected to comply with the following rules and regulations for using the Internet:

1. To use the Internet with the permission of the teacher or staff member in charge. Absolutely NO usage of the Net is allowed without a teacher or staff member present.

2. To use the Internet for educational purposes which are consistent with school policies. Access to sites intended for ADULTS ONLY are prohibited. Any student found accessing a site of this nature will be expelled from using the Internet and/or other appropriate action by school staff.

3. To use the Internet lawfully by not causing personal or financial harm to others.

4. To use the Internet legally by not violating copyright laws.

5. To use the Internet safely by never giving out personal information about yourself, your family or your school. This includes account numbers, telephone numbers and addresses. In some cases, the school address may be used in conjunction with a school project or web page at the discretion of staff.

6. To use the Internet wisely by never sending or keeping messages or data you would not mind having your teacher or your parent read.

7. To use the Internet responsibly by never tampering with hardware or software or vandalizing data.

8. To use the Internet cautiously by not taking chances and by reporting any problems immediately to the teacher or staff member.

Since all of our students are under the age of 18, parental permission [is] required in all cases. Your signature on the attached form indicates that you have read and understand our policy guidelines for Internet access and give permission for your son or daughter to use it.

Name of student (print): _____

Signature of student: _____

Name of parent (print): _____

Signature of parent: _____

Date: _____

DATA COLLECTION
AND ANALYSIS

Ethnographic methods, including participant observation and group and individual interviews, were used in this study to identify, define, and analyze the words and phrases middle school students use to describe their Internet use. Qualitative research is appropriate to study the complex array of changes that may accompany classroom computer use (Papert, 1993, p. 149). As with other technological systems, there is an interdependent relationship between the design and use of the technology and the social system into which it is introduced (Heilbroner, 1967/1994, p. 57). Ethnographic methods allow for discovery of the various levels at which participants interact in a new technological system and provide a means for describing the "subtle but powerful patterns of behavior that characterize social environments such as classrooms" (Windschitl, 1998, p. 31).

Data collection, coding, and analysis were done simultaneously throughout the study (Glaser & Strauss, 1967; Lincoln & Guba, 1985; Spradley, 1980). My data sources included staff interviews, individual and group interviews with students, classroom observations of students working online and offline on projects for which Internet use was required, and an online (Web-based) student discussion of their Internet use. Documents included lesson plans and student research products (papers and Web pages). I relied on classroom observation and a student survey to identify as potential informants students experienced with the Internet.

I conducted student interviews and observations to collect language samples of the words and phrases students use to describe their Internet use. Preliminary analysis revealed that these students had no special lexicon to describe their Internet use. Experienced Internet users in these eighth-grade classes did not distinguish between their online and offline activities and relationships. My focus shifted from the ways in which the students were saying specific words and phrases to the meaning of what they were saying. Subsequent data collection and analysis were designed to answer the question "What do students do on the Internet—that is, what are the activities and relationships students engage in online?" The purpose of the study remained constant: to discover the relationship between students' Internet use and the classroom context. In other words, how do students use the Internet in the midst of the social processes that have evolved over time to support the transmission of knowledge from teacher to students in classrooms and schools?

I coded and analyzed data based on the categories and themes that emerged in the setting. These categories included but were not limited to adults' and students' understanding of the utility of the Internet, classroom instruction and student learning processes as related to Internet skills, adult suspicions of the Internet, and students' own safety precautions. Categories were analyzed for the ways in which perceptions of students and adults converge and diverge. Data collected from staff interviews and classroom observations were coded and analyzed for the technical factors (e.g., computer hardware and software), institutional structures, pedagogy, and social interactions that influence students' Internet use in the classroom.

To gain entry at the level at which students relate to each other required that I win the confidence of the students to communicate with me not just as an adult authority. My goal was to discover how students describe the Internet to their peers and to discourage them from "translating" into terminology they felt an adult would understand (Spradley, 1979, p. 59). At the same time, I needed to maintain a working relationship with the teachers and administrators who had granted me entry into the classroom and retained the right to rescind the permission. This became a delicate balance to maintain. For example, I needed to respond to one teacher's view of me as a "sympathetic ear" to maintain good relations with the staff. I was concerned that students might suspect me of feeding information gained from interviews back to staff. I solved this problem by avoiding conversation with teachers in the presence of students and keeping conversations on friendly or broad professional topics (e.g., upcoming field trips and professional workshops). I never discussed students with the staff.

I changed my attire, speech patterns, and body language to convey to students that I was someone other than a teacher. I realized after an early visit to the school that my blue corduroy skirt and flower-embroidered wool sweater were too close in style to one teacher's plaid skirt and monogrammed Shetland pullover. From that point on, I wore brightly colored jeans, vests, and casual sweaters, which were distinctly different from the teachers' clothing. Students tested my trustworthiness by committing minor infractions of classroom rules and then watching for my reaction. One response I used in these instances was a facial expression of indifference intended to convey my nonjudgmental stance. In the interviews, students' inclusion of anecdotes that they did not want their teachers and parents to know about indicated that I had been successful in earning and maintaining the students' trust.

Language was problematic. When I switched into adolescent language patterns, I was in conflict with the language skills the school sought to cultivate in students. I tried as much as possible to keep separate my interactions with staff and students to minimize the number of times I would need to switch language patterns in any given site visit. In the online discussion, messages fell somewhere between written and spoken communication (Garner & Gillingham, 1996, pp. 8–9). Each message was part of an informal conversation and was converted to text for electronic transmission between participants. The messages became a semipermanent record on the Web-based bulletin board, accessible to students and two teachers. I mixed participants' language and traditional grammar to avoid alienating staff or students who viewed the messages. For example, a question I posted on the Web site discussion read

Sort of related to adult Internet phobias: Yesterday, I heard an adult bashing computers with the comment, "It's hard to curl up with a good CD-ROM." I think the person thinks that books will disappear completely in the future. What do you think?

"Sort of" and "bashing" are not part of my formal speaking or writing. My use of these phrases reflects common language patterns used in conversation by participants. As a researcher, I did not assume that the Internet or any other digital technology should be purchased and maintained by schools. Although I experience the benefits of computers in my own learning, I remain alert to the potential for shifting away from the research role toward advocate for a single technology as the solution for all educational problems (Tennyson, 1994, p. 16). At the same time, I do not assume that schools will continue to exist in their current form as we move into the 21ˢᵗ century. The researcher can acknowledge the changes that accompany the proliferation of digital technology and the shift from industrial to information economy without assigning value to the technology itself.

Agalianos, A. S. (1996, April). *Towards a sociology of educational computing.* Paper presented at the Annual Meeting of the American Educational Research Association, New York, NY. (ERIC Document Reproduction Services No. ED 409 004)

Agalianos, A. S. (1997). *A cultural studies analysis of Logo in education.* Unpublished doctoral dissertation, University of London.

Aspy, D. N. (1986). *This is school! Sit down and listen!* Amherst, MA: Human Resource Development Press.

Bailey, J. (1996). *After thought: The computer challenge to human intelligence.* New York: Basic Books.

Berenstain, S., & Berenstain, J. (1999). *The Berenstain bears lost in cyberspace.* New York: Random House.

Berners-Lee, T. (1996). *The World Wide Web: Past, present and future* [Online]. http://www.w3.org/people/Berners-Lee/1996/ppf.html

Big Picture Geographics (1999). *Latest headcount: 148 million* [Online]. http://cyberatlas.internet.com/big_picture/geographics/article/0,1323,5911_150591,00.html Viewed 6 December 1999.

British Educational Communications and Technology Agency (1998). *National Grid for Learning* [Online]. http://www.ngfl.gov.uk/ Viewed 6 April 2000.

Clinton, W. J. (1997, September 11). *America goes back to school, 1997* [Online]. Federal Register, 62, (176), p. 47909–47912. http://wais.access.gpo.gov [DOCID fr11se97-153].

Cuban, L. (1986). *Teachers and machines: Classroom use of technology since 1920.* New York: Teachers College Press.

Duffy, T. M., & Cunningham, D. J. (1996). Constructivism: Implications for the design and delivery of instruction. In D. H. Jonassen

(Ed.), *Handbook of research for educational communications and technology* (pp. 170–198). New York: Macmillan.

Garner, R., & Gillingham, M. G. (1996). *Internet communication in six classrooms: Conversations across time, space, and culture.* Mahwah, NJ: Erlbaum.

Glaser, B. G., & Strauss, A. L. (1967). *The discovery of grounded theory: Strategies for qualitative research.* New York: Aldine.

Goodlad, J. I. (1984). *A place called school: Prospects for the future.* New York: McGraw-Hill.

Hafner, K., & Lyon, M. (1996). *Where wizards stay up late: The origins of the Internet.* New York: Simon & Schuster.

Harel, I. (1999). *Clickerati kids: Who are they?* [Online]. http://www.mamamedia.com/areas/grownups/new/home.html Viewed 5 December 1999.

Heilbroner, R. L. (1967, 1994). Do machines make history? In M. R. Smith & L. Marx (Eds.), *Does technology drive history? The dilemma of technological determinism* (pp. 53–78). Cambridge, MA: MIT Press.

Honebein, P. C. (1996). Seven goals for the design of constructivist learning environments. In B. Wilson (Ed.), *Constructivist learning environments: Case studies in instructional design.* Englewood Cliffs, NJ: Educational Technology Publication.

Huberman, M. (1983). Recipes for busy kitchens. *Knowledge: Creation, Diffusion, Utilization, 4,* 478–510.

International Education Foundation (1999). *GetNetWise* [Online]. www.getnetwise.org Viewed March 15, 2000

Jerald, C. D. (1998a, October 1). By the numbers. *Education Week, 18*(5), 102–103.

Jerald, C. D. (1998b, October 1). How technology is used. *Education Week, 18*(5), 110–113.

Kay, A. (1998, October). *The role of technology.* Paper presented at the Camden Technology Conference on the Transformation of Learning, Camden, ME.

Kerr, S. T. (1991, Fall). Lever and fulcrum: Educational technology in teachers' thought and practice. *Teachers College Record, 93*(1), 114–136.

Lincoln, Y. S., & Guba, E. G. (1985). *Naturalistic inquiry.* Beverly Hills, CA: Sage.

McCain, J. (1998, February 9). *Internet School Filtering Act.* S. 1619. GPO Access [Online]. http://frwebgate.access.gpo.gov/cgi-bin/useftp.cgi?Ipaddress=162.140.64.21&filename=s1619rs. pdf&directory=/diskb/wais/data/105_cong_bills Viewed March 15, 2000.

Means, B., & Olson, K. (1995, September). *Technology's role in educational reform: Findings from a national study of innovating schools*. Washington, DC: U.S. Department of Education.

Mitchell, W. J. (1995). *City of bits: Space, place, and the Infobahn*. Cambridge, MA: MIT Press.

Navikas, L. (1998, October). *Exploding networks*. Paper presented at the Camden Technology Conference on the Transformation of Learning, Camden, ME.

Negroponte, N. (1995). *Being digital*. New York: Vintage Books.

Olson, J. (1988). *Schoolworlds/Microworlds*. Oxford: Pergamon Press.

Papert, S. (1993). *The children's machine*. New York: Basic Books.

Papert, S. (1996). *The connected family: Bridging the digital generation gap*. Atlanta: Longstreet Press.

Papert, S. (1998, October). *Targets hit; targets missed*. Paper presented at the Camden Technology Conference on the Transformation of Learning, Camden, ME.

Perkins, D. (1992). Technology meets constructivism: Do they make a marriage? In T. Duffy & D. Jonassen (Eds.), *Constructivism and the technology of instruction: A conversation*. Hillsdale, NJ: Erlbaum.

Resnick, M. (1994/1997). *Turtles, termites, and traffic jams: Explorations in massively parallel microworlds*. Cambridge, MA: MIT Press.

Sarason, S. B. (1996). *Revisiting "The Culture of the School and the Problem of Change."* New York: Teachers College Press.

Savery, J., & Duffy, T. (1996). Problem based learning: An instructional model and its constructivist framework. In B. Wilson (Ed.), *Constructivist learning environments: Case studies in instructional design*. Englewood Cliffs, NJ: Educational Technology Publication.

Schofield, J. W. (1996). *Computers and classroom culture*. Cambridge, England: Cambridge University Press.

Sitton, T. (1980, April). Inside school spaces: Rethinking the hidden dimension. *Urban Education, 15*(1), 65–82.

Sizer, T. R. (1984). *Horace's compromise: The dilemma of the American high school*. Boston: Houghton Mifflin.

Spradley, J. P. (1979). *The ethnographic interview*. New York: Harcourt Brace Jovanovich.

Spradley, J. P. (1980). *Participant observation*. New York: Holt, Rinehart & Winston.

Stevens, E. W., Jr. (1995). *The grammar of the machine: Technical literacy and early industrial expansion in the United States.* New Haven, CT: Yale University Press.

Stone, L. (1998, October). *Reaching adults.* Paper presented at the Camden Technology Conference on the Transformation of Learning, Camden, ME.

Tapscott, D. (1998). *Growing up digital: The rise of the Net Generation.* New York: McGraw-Hill.

Tennyson, R. (1994). The big wrench vs. integrated approaches: The great media debate. *Education Technology Research & Development, 42*(3), 15–28.

Tiffin, J., & Rajasingham, L. (1995). *In search of the virtual class.* New York: Routledge.

Turkle, S. (1995). *Life on the screen: Identity in the age of the Internet.* New York: Simon & Schuster.

Tyack, D., & Tobin, W. (1994, Fall). The "Grammar" of schooling: Why has it been so hard to change? *American Educational Research Journal, 31*(3), 453–479.

Vickers, M., & Smalley, J. (1995). Integrating computers into classroom teaching: Cross-national perspectives. In D. M. Perkins et al. (Eds.), *Software goes to school: Teaching for understanding with new technologies* (pp. 271–282). New York: Oxford University Press.

von Glaserfeld, E. (1996). Introduction: Aspects of constructivism. In C. Fosnot (Ed.), *Constructivism: Theory, perspectives and practice.* New York: Teachers College Press.

Windschitl, M. (1998, January/February). The WWW and classroom research: What path should we take? *Educational Researcher, 27*(1), 28–33.

Wiske, M. S., & Houde, R. (1988). From recitation to construction: Teachers change with new technologies. In J. Schwartz, M. Yerushalmy, & B. Wilson (Eds.), *The Geometric Supposer: What is it a case of?* (pp. 193–215). Hillsdale, NJ: Erlbaum.

Zhao, Y. (1998, Spring). Design for adoption: The development of an integrated Web-based education environment. *Journal of Research on Computing in Education, 30*(3), 307–328.

Radio, 15, 23, 106
Real, 47
Recitation model, 29–30, 34, 38,
    39–40
Research. *See* Students, research;
    Students, research papers
Resnick, Mitchel, 18
Richardson, Lewis, 18
Role playing games. *See* Games,
    role playing

Safety. *See* Internet, safety
School. *See also* Classroom
    as physical entity, 18–19, 32–33
    purpose of, 13, 30–31, 33
    schedule, 24, 30, 37, 148
    university partnerships, 6, 40
Scotland, 37
Screen names, 17, 52–53, 101, 120.
    See also Anonymity;
    Facelessness
Search engines, 81, 86–88, 92
Searching. *See* Information, searching
Security, network. *See* Networks,
    security
Servers. *See* Web servers
Sesame Street, 20
Shopping. *See* Internet, shopping
Shopping malls, 58, 62, 93
Sports Illustrated, 110
StarLogo (programming
    language), 18
Student–teacher relationship, 30,
    35, 37–38, 39, 124, 133,
    137, 148–149, 150, 152
Students. *See also* Student–teacher
    relationship
    daily activities, 10, 67, 107
    Internet experience, 10, 16,
    43–44, 67, 107–108,
    117–118, 123–124, 150
    research, 8, 22, 72, 76, 77,
    78, 85

research papers, 72, 78, 114,
    129, 132–133, 148
role in classroom, 11–12, 15,
    29, 30, 37–39, 124, 133,
    135, 137, 143–144,
    148–149, 150, 151, 152
as teachers, 144, 148, 150
Synchronous. *See* Communication,
    synchronous

Teachers. *See also* Student–teacher
    relationship
    authority of, 150
    control by, 38
    as Internet users, 12, 77,
    106–108, 147, 150,
    152–153, 154,
    156–157, 160
    as learners, 12, 148, 151,
    156, 160
    motivation to use
    technology, 36
    pedagogical beliefs, 34–35
    power, 35
    professional development, 12,
    147, 152, 158, 159–160
    role in classroom, 15, 30, 35,
    37–38, 39, 123–124, 130,
    135, 143–144, 150
    as technology pioneers, 36–37
Technical support, 158–159
    online, 64–65
    in schools, 29
Technology integration, 148, 157
Telephone, 4, 20, 60, 93, 97,
    108, 113
Television, 2, 3–4, 15, 58, 106
Tests. *See* Assessment, tests
Textbooks, 16, 30, 69–70, 133,
    151, 153
Transparency of technology, 44,
    47–48
Typing. *See* Keyboard skills